Feeding Anxiety to Your Kids

Exploring Parental Anxiety and Its Intergenerational Transmission

Dr Bandara Bandaranayake, PhD

ISBN: 978-0-6452133-6-2

Email: bandaranayakeb@gmail.com

Publisher: Bandaranayake Consulting Services Pty Ltd

Melbourne, Australia

Dedication

To My Grandchildren:

Kiran, Arjun, & Asha

What This Book Is All About

───── ꙩ ⚜ ꙩ ─────

Are you unknowingly passing your anxiety to your children?

Have you ever wondered how your parents' anxiety may have influenced you?

✧ *Discover the hidden ways anxiety is transmitted across generations.*

✧ *Uncover the critical times and stages when children are most vulnerable.*

✧ *Discover your innate mind power and explore deliberate strategies to break free from the cycle of anxiety.*

Feeding Anxiety to Your Kids uncovers the often-overlooked phenomenon of how parental anxiety is transmitted to children, profoundly shaping their emotional and psychological development. Drawing from extensive clinical experience with adolescents struggling with severe anxiety, panic attacks, and self-harming behaviors, this book reveals how parental anxiety can subtly but significantly influence children's well-being and affect family dynamics across generations.

This publication offers a well-rounded understanding and multifaceted nature of anxiety. By integrating cutting-edge research in evolutionary psychology, neurobiology, and psychodynamics with real-life examples from clinical practice, the book provides readers with deep insights into the origins of parental anxiety and its far-reaching consequences. It highlights critical life stages—pregnancy, early childhood, and adolescence—when children are particularly vulnerable to absorbing anxiety. The book examines how dysregulated behaviors like overprotection, hypervigilance, catastrophic thinking, emotional unavailability, and inconsistent parenting unintentionally perpetuate anxiety, while also exploring the broader intergenerational and multigenerational impacts.

Feeding Anxiety to Your Kids offers a hopeful and proactive approach, emphasising that effective strategies and tools are available to break the cycle of anxiety. It serves as a call to deliberate action for parents, caregivers, therapists, and health professionals, providing practical strategies, actionable insights, and encouragement to nurture emotionally secure and resilient families. Whether you are a parent navigating personal challenges, a professional supporting family, or an individual seeking to understand anxiety's complexities, this book delivers a comprehensive blend of knowledge and optimism for fostering a healthier, brighter future for generations to come.

Table of Contents

Acknowledgements

I acknowledge many people who aided in this publication.

Firstly, I would like to extend my heartfelt gratitude to the many adolescents and their parents who participated in psychotherapy sessions over the years. Your courage, openness, and willingness to share your emotions and stories provided invaluable insights and deeply informed the development of this book.

Special thanks go to Dr. Chamara Basnayake, Associate Professor (Clinical) at St Vincent's Hospital, University of Melbourne, and Dr. Surabhi Kumble Basnayake, General Practitioner, for their thoughtful comments and constructive feedback. Your expertise and input were instrumental in refining the content and addressing key challenges in this complex subject area.

I am also profoundly grateful to Tony Gilmore, Psychotherapist at Whole Mind Strategies, Dandenong, for his valuable feedback on the first draft. Your insights and suggestions significantly improved the clarity and depth of this work.

Additionally, I would like to acknowledge the many friends, colleagues, and professionals who offered their support, encouragement, and expertise throughout the writing process.

Finally, I would like to express my heartfelt appreciation to the readers of this book. Your interest in understanding and addressing the complex dynamics of parental anxiety inspires me to continue exploring and contributing to this important field. Thank you for joining me on this journey toward greater awareness and healing.

Your feedback and comments are deeply valued and greatly appreciated.

Part One:

Setting the Scene

Chapter 1:

Introduction and Book Roadmap

The primary goal of this book is to provide a comprehensive understanding of how parental anxiety is transmitted to children and its intergenerational impact. It seeks to shed light on a largely unrecognised and underexplored process that profoundly affects not only the emotional and psychological development of children but also the overall dynamics of the family and across generations.

As a psychotherapist, I have worked with numerous families where parental anxiety played a significant role in shaping the emotional development of children and influencing family welfare. Many parents sought my help for their children—particularly adolescents struggling with severe anxiety, panic attacks, self-harming tendencies, or academic and behavioural issues. What often became evident through these interactions, and what anecdotal evidence strongly suggested, was that the anxiety experienced by these children was not isolated to them. In many cases, both parents were grappling with deep-seated anxiety, frequently undiagnosed or unacknowledged, which had a profound impact on the emotional well-being of the entire family.

In order to understand the broader issue about intergenerational anxiety transmission this book is grounded in both theory and practice. It draws upon established research in evolutionary psychology, neurobiology, psychodynamics, cognitive-behavioural, and sociocultural models. By integrating these theoretical frameworks with real-world clinical observations, the book provides a comprehensive awareness of anxiety and its transmission.

What is anxiety?

Before diving deeply into the subject matter of this book, it is essential to establish a comprehensive understanding of anxiety. What exactly is anxiety?

Anxiety, from a conventional psychological perspective, is defined as an emotional response characterised by worry, tension, and a range of physical symptoms such as increased heart rate, restlessness, and hypervigilance. It is considered pathological when it becomes excessive, persistent, or disproportionate to the actual threat, disrupting daily functioning. Key aspects of anxiety include cognitive patterns like rumination or catastrophic thinking, emotional feelings of unease, physical symptoms such as trembling or gastrointestinal distress, panic attacks, and avoidance behaviors. These features form the basis for diagnosing anxiety disorders, such as generalised anxiety disorder or phobias, as outlined in the Diagnostic and Statistical Manual of Mental Disorders (5th ed., DSM-5; American Psychiatric Association, 2013).

In contrast, the evolutionary psychological perspective frames anxiety as adaptive mechanisms that evolved to enhance survival. Anxiety functions as a "threat detection system," enabling individuals to detect and respond to potential dangers in ancestral environments, such as anticipating predators or navigating social conflicts. This system promotes vigilance and protective behaviors, which historically enhanced fitness by increasing the likelihood of survival. Similarly, low mood serves an adaptive function by conserving energy and reducing exposure to harm during periods when action would be fruitless or risky. As explored by Marks and Nesse (1994) and Nesse (2001, 2022), the prevalence of anxiety reflects its historical role in promoting survival, even if its overactivation now leads to dysfunction.

However, these adaptive mechanisms can become maladaptive in modern environments due to evolutionary mismatches. The chronic stressors of contemporary society—such as prolonged goal pursuit, work-related pressures, relationship issues, and health issues—can lead to persistent or exaggerated activation of anxiety and depressive responses. This dysregulation transforms protective systems into sources of significant distress, resulting in clinical disorders. Anxiety, for example, may produce excessive or unwarranted vigilance, akin to a "smoke detector" that frequently produces false alarms to avoid missing potential threats. Similarly, depression may manifest as prolonged low mood that undermines functionality rather than conserving energy. These mismatches highlight the need to understand mental illnesses not as purely maladaptive but as evolved responses that have become unsuited to current environmental conditions.

In essence, anxiety is an adaptive safety mechanism that evolved to enhance survival by alerting individuals to potential threats. However, when anxiety becomes persistently or excessively activated, it can become dysregulated, leading to chronic stress and depressive responses that significantly impair quality of life.

This publication refers to a range of major forms of anxiety, including Generalised Anxiety Disorder (GAD), Social Anxiety Disorder (SAD), panic disorder (PD), Post-Traumatic Stress Disorder (PTSD), and Obsessive Compulsive Disorder (OCD). Specific to mothers, the focus extends to forms of anxiety such as Prenatal Anxiety, Postpartum Anxiety, Separation Anxiety, and Maternal Performance Anxiety. These types of anxiety are introduced in detail in Chapter Three.

The Cost of Anxiety to Human Lifespan

Anxiety disorders are among the most prevalent mental health conditions globally and in Australia, with significant implications for maternal health. As of 2019, approximately 301 million people worldwide were living with an anxiety disorder, accounting for about 4.05% of the global population. (Javaid, S.F. et al. 2023). In Australia, anxiety disorders are the most common mental health conditions. Data from the Australian Bureau of Statistics' National Study of Mental Health and Wellbeing (2020–2022) indicates that 17.2% of Australians aged 16–85 years experienced an anxiety disorder in the previous 12 months. This translates to approximately 3.4 million people. The prevalence is notably higher among females (21.0%) compared to males (12.4%). Young adults aged 16–24 years also exhibit higher rates, with 31.5% experiencing an anxiety disorder in the past year.

Worldwide, 10% to 20% of women experience anxiety during pregnancy or postpartum (WHO, 2022) Maternal anxiety, particularly during the perinatal period, is a significant concern in Australia. Studies have found that anxiety disorders affect approximately 10% to 20% of mothers during pregnancy and the postpartum period with an increasing trend (AIHW, 2024, Dennis et al. 2017).

Anxiety can impose significant costs on human lifespan by contributing to chronic stress, which disrupts key physiological systems. Prolonged activation of the hypothalamic-pituitary-adrenal (HPA) axis leads to elevated cortisol levels, increasing the risk of cardiovascular diseases, immune dysfunction, and metabolic disorders like diabetes. Anxiety is also linked to unhealthy coping behaviors, such as substance abuse and poor sleep, which further degrade health.

Additionally, chronic anxiety affects mental well-being, increasing the likelihood of depression and social isolation, both of which are associated with reduced lifespan. The cumulative impact of physiological stress and behavioural factors accelerates aging processes, such as cellular inflammation and telomere shortening, ultimately reducing overall longevity.

Parental Role – A Context

Since this publication is centred on the transmission of parental anxiety to children it is important to understand the maternal and paternal roles within a family structure where the children are grown.

The parental behavior is fundamentally directed at enhancing the survival and development of offspring, adapting widely across species due to ecological and evolutionary pressures. Mammals rely heavily on parental care, making it a critical component of their offspring's survival strategies (Numan & Insel, 2003). In most mammalian species, particularly polygynous or promiscuous ones, caregiving is predominantly maternal and driven by lactation (Lukas & Clutton-Brock, 2013). Humans primarily exhibit social monogamy with 80-85% of marriages worldwide adhering to this norm (Henrich, Boyd, & Richerson, 2012).

Monogamy, whether genetic or social, provides valuable insights into parental behavior. In socially monogamous species, biparental care is often observed, with shared caregiving enhancing offspring survival (Numan, 2016). However, maternal care typically remains predominant, even in socially monogamous mammals, due to the physiological demands of lactation. Consequently, it is reasonable to consider that the maternal role is essential to the physical and emotional development of a human child, particularly during the early stages of life.

Fathers complement maternal roles by encouraging exploration, social learning, and resilience. They engage in stimulating play and risk-taking behaviors, promoting problem-solving skills and adaptability. Fathers also model social behaviors, such as conflict management and boundary-setting, teaching children's societal norms and emotional expression (Buss, 1989).

The interplay of maternal and paternal roles evolves as children grow. Mothers' caregiving forms the foundation of emotional development in early stages, while fathers' influence grows, shaping social behaviors and external adaptability. Together, their contributions supposed to create a balanced framework for nurturing emotional security and resilience, reflecting an evolutionary strategy of shared responsibility (Paquette, 2004; Lamb, M. (Ed.) 2010)

However, maladaptive parental roles and mechanisms can become dysregulated, resulting in excessive worry and overprotective behaviors that may inadvertently foster anxiety, which can be transmitted to children.

Evolving Motherhood Role in Modern Society

Mothers have become central decision-makers in modern families, taking on roles that extend beyond their biological bond through lactation and caregiving to include strategic decisions that shape their family's future. These responsibilities often encompass critical areas such as housing, education, healthcare, and the overall development of their children. Driven by the philosophy of "intensive mothering" (Hays, 1996), mothers prioritise creating environments that nurture their children's physical, emotional, and intellectual growth. Research highlights that mothers frequently take the lead in securing the best opportunities for their children, such as researching schools, engaging with teachers, and planning extracurricular activities (Schneider et al., 2006).

While these efforts demonstrate mothers' deep commitment to their children's success, they also place immense pressure on themselves to meet societal and self-imposed expectations. This persistent pressure often amplifies maternal anxiety, resulting in decision fatigue, feelings of guilt, and a pervasive sense of inadequacy. The dual burden of fulfilling caregiving duties while navigating complex strategic responsibilities underscores the emotional challenges many mothers face in modern family dynamics.

The Transmission of Anxiety

The transmission of anxiety from parents to children is a multifaceted process influenced by biological mechanisms, environmental factors, and caregiving behaviors. Maternal behavior, foundational to attachment and caregiving, is regulated by subcortical brain regions such as the medial preoptic area (MPOA), amygdala, and nucleus accumbens, which drive maternal instincts, emotional processing, and caregiving motivation. Infant cues like crying or laughter activate these neural systems, stimulating the maternal reward pathways via dopaminergic mechanisms. Higher-order brain regions, including the medial prefrontal cortex (mPFC) and anterior cingulate cortex (ACC), further enhance maternal sensitivity by enabling nuanced interpretation of infant emotional states. Oxytocin, a key bonding hormone, bolsters maternal sensitivity and emotional warmth, while neuroplastic changes during pregnancy and postpartum optimise caregiving behaviors to support infant survival and emotional development (Bowlby, 1969; Meaney, 2001).

Parental anxiety, including maternal anxiety, can influence developmental processes in both prenatal and postnatal environments. Elevated maternal cortisol levels during pregnancy, often a result of chronic stress, may impact fetal development, increasing a child's stress reactivity and susceptibility to anxiety (O'Donnell et al., 2009). Postnatally, behaviors such as heightened vigilance or overprotection, often stemming from maternal anxiety, may present challenges to secure attachment formation and emotional regulation. However, it is important to recognise that such behaviors may have been adaptive in high-threat ancestral environments, as suggested by Bowlby's attachment theory, and are not a reflection of personal inadequacy.

Fathers play a complementary role in caregiving, supported by neural circuits such as the MPOA and nucleus accumbens. Hormonal changes, including increased oxytocin and decreased testosterone levels, enhance paternal sensitivity and nurturing behaviors, contributing to a balanced parental dynamic that fosters emotional security and resilience.

Children exposed to chronic parental anxiety often internalise their parents' distress, leading to emotional dysregulation, heightened stress sensitivity, and difficulties managing fear or worry. Anxious parenting fosters insecure attachments, creating an unstable environment that compromises a child's sense of safety. This dynamic may manifest behaviourally as social withdrawal, excessive dependence, or aggression, mirroring the anxious responses modelled by parents. Over time, these patterns reinforce negative cognitive biases and hyperawareness of threats, increasing the likelihood of anxiety disorders, depression, and other mental health challenges in children.

Factors Beyond Parental Role

I am not suggesting that all the children develop anxiety condition solely due to their parents. After all anxiety is a maladaptation response to environmental stimuli. In many cases, environmental factors—such as unexpected or prolonged emotional stressors, trauma, or significant life events, peer pressure—play a major role in the onset of anxiety. These external circumstances can disrupt a child's emotional development and natural healing processes, making it more difficult for them to recover from early emotional challenges. It is recognised that external influences, beyond parental interactions, can significantly shape a child's ability to cope with stress and impact their long-term emotional well-being.

The Impact of Intergenerational Anxiety

This publication primarily focuses on the transmission of intergenerational anxiety. However, anxiety transmission can occur both intergenerationally and multi-generationally, depending on the context and underlying mechanisms. While the terms are often used interchangeably, they have distinct meanings.

Intergenerational Transmission refers to the direct transfer of anxiety from one generation to the next, typically from parent to child. This transmission occurs through mechanisms such as biological influences (e.g., genetic predispositions), behavioural patterns (e.g., learned responses to stress), and environmental factors (e.g., family dynamics or stress-inducing settings).

Multigenerational Transmission refers to the broader and more extended transmission of anxiety across multiple generations. This occurs through cumulative effects, such as persistent family patterns of anxiety or trauma; socio-cultural influences, including cultural norms and values shaped by historical experiences; and epigenetic changes, where trauma or stress experienced by one generation leaves biological imprints that affect future generations.

In summary, intergenerational transmission focuses on the direct parent-to-child dynamic, while multigenerational transmission encompasses the broader influence of family history, cultural context, and inherited biological changes across generations. Both perspectives are essential for a comprehensive understanding of how anxiety is transmitted.

Parental Anxiety in Modern Family Dynamics

In addition to traditional nuclear family structures, modern society includes a variety of family dynamics, such as single-parent households, divorced families, and families with LGBTQ+ parents. These diverse family structures offer unique parenting roles and experiences, which can shape children's emotional development in distinct ways. While these dynamics may present specific challenges, they also bring opportunities for fostering resilience, adaptability, and strong emotional bonds, all of which influence children's vulnerability to anxiety.

Divorce often creates a period of upheaval and adjustment for children, leading to heightened anxiety. Changes in family dynamics, routines, and living arrangements can disrupt a child's sense of stability and security. According to Amato (2000), children from divorced families are more likely to exhibit elevated levels of anxiety and depression compared to their peers from intact families, particularly during the initial years following the separation. Contributing factors include ongoing parental disputes, diminished parental time, and economic hardships that can add to the stress burden on children.

Children in single-parent families may also encounter challenges that elevate their risk of anxiety, such as reduced parental support, societal stigma and financial instability. Single parents, often juggling multiple roles, may experience stress spillover, which children can perceive and internalise. However, not all children in single-parent households experience anxiety.

Children raised in LGBT families are not inherently more prone to anxiety than their peers from heterosexual families.

However, external factors such as societal stigma and discrimination toward LGBT parents can indirectly contribute to anxiety. Research by Bos et al. (2007) indicates that children from LGBT families experience comparable psychological outcomes to those from heterosexual families when parental warmth, stability, and emotional support are present. Key factors influencing anxiety in children from LGBT families include social stigma, peer rejection, and parental stress, which can heighten feelings of vulnerability.

Positive Outlook - Anxiety Treatment

This publication does not portray anxiety as an insurmountable crisis but instead highlights the hope provided by modern treatment models. While recognising the harmful effects of dysregulated anxiety, it emphasises the effectiveness of contemporary interventions, particularly those informed by evolutionary psychology. Understanding anxiety from this perspective enables clinicians to recalibrate the brain's alarm system, addressing both symptoms and underlying environmental and behavioural triggers.

For non-complex anxiety disorders such as generalised anxiety disorder (GAD) or specific phobias, treatment is often highly effective, with evidence-based approaches like Cognitive Behavioural Therapy (CBT) and Mindfulness-Based Stress Reduction (MBSR) showing significant improvements within 6–12 weeks, and full remission within 3–6 months. In contrast, complex anxiety disorders, particularly those linked to trauma, comorbid conditions like depression or OCD, or chronic patterns, require multimodal, trauma-informed approaches. These cases often take 12–24 months or longer for substantial improvement, with ongoing therapy needed to sustain progress.

Medical interventions have also advanced in identifying and addressing underlying organic causes of anxiety and managing severe episodes of dysregulation. These treatments are most effective when integrated with psychotherapy, lifestyle adjustments, and stress management techniques, forming a comprehensive approach to mental health care.

However, prevention remains more effective than cure. Targeted early interventions at key life stages, along with supportive social welfare policies, can significantly reduce the prevalence of anxiety disorders. Special attention should be given to young married couples, pregnancy periods, and at-risk groups, such as individuals affected by family violence or trauma. While this publication does not propose policy-level strategies, it underscores the importance of preventive measures in mitigating anxiety's long-term impact.

Book Structure and Organisation of Chapters

This book is structured into seven comprehensive parts, each exploring different dimensions of parental anxiety, its transmission, and its impact, with the final part focusing on recovery prospects. The content is deliberately designed to highlight the interconnections and overlaps that underpin the central theme of parental anxiety under different dimensions. As a result, each chapter contains valuable insights that can also be understood and appreciated individually.

Part One comprises three chapters. The opening chapter (present chapter) outlines the book's purpose and scope. Chapter Two presents real-life examples from my work with adolescents, highlighting the effects of parental anxiety on their emotional well-being. Chapter Three categorises various forms of anxiety using contemporary medical terminology.

Part Two provides a conceptual foundation across six chapters. Chapter Four discusses infants' vulnerability and their dependence on primary caregivers for suvival and development. Chapter Five explores the genetic and environmental factors contributing to anxiety, including epigenetics. Chapter Six examines anxiety as a learned behavior, reinforced through daily interactions and observed family behaviors. Chapter Seven delves into the evolutionary origins of anxiety, offering a theoretical perspective. Chapter Eight focuses on the brain's role in processing perceived threats, particularly the amygdala, and aligns these processes with Choice Theory.

Part Three contains two chapters. Chapter Nine identifies behaviors and personality traits exhibited by parents with severe anxiety. Chapter Ten explores the subtle transmission of anxiety from parents to children, encompassing both biological and emotional pathways, such as emotional mirroring and imitation.

Part Four covers the critical periods of pregnancy, birth, and early childhood across four chapters. Chapter Eleven examines how maternal anxiety during pregnancy affects fetal development through biological and emotional channels. Chapter Twelve investigates the impact of C-sections and induced labour on maternal mental health and early bonding, potentially fostering anxiety in children. Chapter Thirteen discusses the effects of postpartum anxiety on emotional bonding and the long-term development of the child. Chapter Fourteen analyses the role of the mother as the primary caregiver, shaped by biological, social, cultural, and legal factors.

Part Five addresses the early roots of anxiety in three chapters. Chapter Fifteen explores the initial development of emotional patterns that may persist into later life. Chapter Sixteen identifies periods when children are most susceptible to anxiety, noting that a significant portion of personality development occurs by age seven. Chapter Seventeen discusses attachment theory, various attachment styles, and the long-term consequences of insecure attachments, linking early experiences to maladaptive behaviors in adulthood.

Part Six examines family dynamics in four chapters. Chapter Eighteen investigates the influence of anxious grandparents in multigenerational contexts, especially in culturally diverse families in Western societies. Chapter Nineteen explores how parents' unmet needs and unresolved fears may lead them to project anxieties onto their children. Chapter Twenty analyses how parental anxiety can contribute to family and relationship breakdowns. Chapter Twenty-One delves into the repercussions of family violence on children's emotional development and mental health.

Part Seven, the final part, offers strategies to break the cycle of anxiety in four chapters. Chapter Twenty-Two highlights the body's natural capacity to heal from anxiety. Chapter Twenty-Three discusses deliberate actions beyond natural healing mechanisms to address anxiety. Chapter Twenty-Four identifies critical life stages suitable for proactive interventions to mitigate anxiety. Chapter Twenty-Five concludes by emphasising the importance of awareness regarding parental anxiety and its intergenerational transmission, advocating for deliberate actions to achieve a quality life.

Chapter 2:

Observing Anxious Parents in Action

———— ❧ ————

This chapter offers anecdotal evidence and observations gathered through my practice to develop and test assumptions, conduct research, and examine the relationship between parental anxiety and childhood anxiety. The purpose of presenting this information is to enhance the validity and reliability of the subject matter and support the direction of this publication.

Authors Experience and Encounters

Throughout my years as a psychotherapist, I have encountered numerous families where parental anxiety, particularly maternal anxiety, played a significant yet often unspoken role in shaping family dynamics. Many of these parents came to me seeking help for their children—adolescents who were experiencing severe anxiety, panic attacks, self-harm tendencies, or behavioural challenges. After a couple of sessions with adolescents, I usually conduct at least one session with the parents for more exploration of the family dynamics in which the kids' anxiety has developed and further sustained. In these cases, what often became apparent was that the anxiety wasn't limited to the child. The parents, too, were grappling with a deep-seated anxiety, often undiagnosed and unacknowledged.

Parental anxiety often presents itself through a mix of emotional and behavioural signs that can deeply impact both the parents and their children. These parents were often unaware that their anxiety was impacting their children. Many therapy sessions failed to transition into family therapy or to encourage the parents to seek help. This reluctance or inability to recognise the problem largely rested with the parents, making progress in therapy more challenging.

Unrecognised Anxiety in Mothers

One case stands out. A mother came to me with concerns about her 14-year-old daughter, who had recently started experiencing insecurity, fear, lack of confidence, panic attacks and was cutting herself as a way to cope. In our initial session, the mother's focus was entirely on her daughter's unusual behaviours. As the sessions progressed, it became clear that this mother had been battling her own anxiety for years, managing her stress by trying to control every aspect of her daughter's life. She had a constant fear that something would go wrong—whether it was related to her daughter's safety, her schoolwork, or her friendships.

This fear drove her to monitor her daughter's every move, constantly checking in with her, imposing strict rules, and second-guessing her decisions. Over time, her daughter had absorbed this anxiety, feeling suffocated by her mother's overprotectiveness, and ultimately internalising her mother's fears. The daughter's self-harming and panic attacks were not isolated behaviors but rather symptoms of the deep-rooted anxiety she had absorbed from her mother. This anxiety was compounded by the absence of a supportive and enriching family environment, which left her without the emotional resources necessary to cope effectively. Her struggles were an outward manifestation of internalised stress and fear, illustrating the profound impact of maternal anxiety on the child's emotional well-being.

Manifestations of Anxiety in Family Dynamics

What struck me in cases was how subtle maternal anxiety could be—and how easily it went unnoticed. Parents often didn't realise how their own emotional states were influencing their children. It wasn't always overt panic or clear signs of distress that indicated parental anxiety. Instead, it was the constant "what ifs," the silent but pervasive worries about every detail of their child's life, the excessive need for control, and the fear of things falling apart that created an anxious environment.

In another case, a mother came to therapy with her teenage son, who was struggling with school refusal and social isolation. In our sessions, I noticed how she would speak for her son, answering questions on his behalf, often framing his experiences through the lens of her own worries. The mother was clearly anxious about her son's future— whether he would be able to succeed academically, make friends, or find a place in the world. She believed that by stepping in and taking control, she could protect him from failure or disappointment.

However, her son felt increasingly powerless and lacked self confidence and freedom, as though he couldn't make decisions for himself without disappointing his mother. He had learned to avoid challenges because, in his eyes, failure would validate his mother's worst fears.

A Case of Social Anxiety

A 17-year-old secondary school student, presented with debilitating social anxiety that significantly impacted his academic performance, peer relationships, and daily functioning. He reported an intense fear of social interactions, particularly speaking in front of others, which led to avoidance behaviors such as skipping classes and declining invitations to social events. During initial therapy sessions, he described persistent feelings of inadequacy and a fear of being judged or humiliated. His symptoms included physical manifestations such as sweating, trembling, and nausea in social situations. Despite his high academic potential, this child had withdrawn from extracurricular activities and displayed signs of emotional distress, including irritability and low self-esteem.

This child's family history revealed a strong link to his condition. His father, who struggled with depression, often displayed emotional withdrawal and limited engagement with the family. This left the youngster feeling unsupported and uncertain about his role in the family dynamic. Meanwhile, his mother suffered from severe anxiety, frequently exhibiting worry and hypervigilance. She often projected her fears onto the youngster, expressing excessive concern about his safety and performance, which created a constant environment of stress and heightened expectations. The parents' struggles not only affected the child's emotional development but also contributed to a deteriorating family relationship characterised by conflict, avoidance, and a lack of effective communication. John internalised his mother's anxious worldview and his father's disengagement, shaping his own perception of the world as threatening and unpredictable.

A Case of Feeling Not Good Enough

A 16-year-old high school female student sought therapy due to feelings of inadequacy, a lack of trust in others, and avoidance of social relationships. During initial sessions, the student described pervasive self-doubt and a belief that she was "never good enough." She avoided forming close friendships and withdrew from social gatherings, fearing judgment and rejection. The student also reported an intense preoccupation with her appearance, frequently checking mirrors, and changing outfits multiple times before leaving home, which further contributed to her anxiety and isolation.

The student's difficulties were deeply rooted in her relationship with her mother, who struggled with severe anxiety and body image concerns. Throughout the girl's childhood, her mother often made comments about her weight, describing her as "fat" or "chubby," and frequently remarked that no dress would fit her properly. Her mother's anxiety-driven perfectionism and critical comments created an environment of constant scrutiny, leading the student to internalise feelings of shame and inadequacy about her body and worth. The mother's habit of changing her own clothes repeatedly before leaving the house set an example that reinforced the belief that appearance dictated social acceptance and self-value.

Unfulfilled Dreams and Social Acceptance

I worked with a teenager facing severe anxiety, primarily caused by the immense pressure from her parents to pursue a prestigious career in medicine. This pressure stemmed from the parents' unmet ambitions and their comparisons to other families whose children were thriving in high-status professions. Desiring validation and a sense of achievement through their child, the parents struggled to accept the teenager's passion for becoming a refugee welfare advocate—a path the teenager found deeply meaningful and personally fulfilling. Although both careers focus on helping vulnerable populations and providing healing, the parents value system, fixated on financial success and social status, blinded her to the worth of her child's chosen career.

This ongoing conflict between the teenager's personal aspirations and the parents' expectations led to growing frustration, helplessness, and chronic anxiety in the child. The teenager felt trapped, torn between wanting to meet their parents' approval and pursuing their true passion. This internal struggle manifested in severe stress, including frequent panic attacks, difficulty focusing in school, and persistent feelings of inadequacy. The relationships became problematic. The parents' inability to recognise and support their child's chosen path not only exacerbated the teenager's anxiety but also led the child to question their own self-worth and potential, further deepening the emotional toll.

The Hidden Transmission of Anxiety

One of the most striking patterns I observed was how often parents' anxiety was passed on to their children without them even realising it. This transmission didn't occur through words but rather through the atmosphere they created within the family. Children absorb their parents' fears, not just through direct communication, but through body language, tone of voice, and emotional responses to everyday situations. A parent's anxious response to a minor accident, a sudden shift in routine, or a difficult decision signals to the child that the world is unpredictable and potentially dangerous. Over time, this repeated exposure to parental anxiety shapes the child's worldview.

For example, I worked with a 14-year-old son was experiencing debilitating social anxiety. The boy had become withdrawn, refusing to participate in school activities or social gatherings. Through our sessions, we discovered that the parents had their own deep-rooted anxieties about social situations, though they hadn't realised how much it affected their son. When their son was younger, they had avoided taking him to birthday parties, large gatherings, or social events because they made the parents uncomfortable. The family had no parties, home gatherings or attending social events. The parents believed that by protecting him from these situations, they were keeping him safe. However, the child had internalised this avoidance as fear, learning to see social interactions as inherently threatening.

Perspectives on my Observations

The cases discussed in this chapter offer anecdotal insights into how parental anxiety affects children. While not exhaustive, these examples highlight key patterns observed during my work with families.

Many parents focus intensely on their children's needs, often neglecting their own emotional health. This oversight can lead to unresolved anxieties subtly influencing their children's emotional development. By not addressing their internal struggles, parents may inadvertently perpetuate cycles of stress within the household.

A common observation is parents' reluctance to seek professional help, believing that prioritising their children means sacrificing their own well-being. Cultural and societal norms often reinforce this belief, portraying a "good parent" as one who neglects personal needs for the family's sake. This mindset undervalues self-care, allowing unresolved emotional issues to persist and subtly affect children. Some parents also view seeking help as an unnecessary expense, not recognising it as a critical investment in their family's long-term happiness and stability.

Chapter 3:

Understanding Anxiety: Forms and Types

This chapter defines the terminology associated with various recognised forms and types of anxiety, offering clarity and consistency for the diverse usage of anxiety-related terms throughout the publication.

Normal Anxiety

Normal anxiety is a natural and adaptive response to potential threats, essential for survival, as it helps individuals cope with challenges or avoid harm through proportional physiological and emotional changes. This temporary response resolves once the threat or challenge has passed, enhancing alertness, focus, and decision-making. Key features include its adaptive purpose, aiding preparation for challenges like public speaking or avoiding harm, and its context-appropriate intensity that matches the level of threat. Anxiety activates the sympathetic nervous system, triggering the fight-or-flight response, which improves readiness in dangerous or high-stakes situations. For instance, feeling nervous before an exam motivates preparation, while anxiety when walking alone at night fosters caution and vigilance.

Disordered Anxiety

Disordered anxiety occurs when the mechanisms regulating anxiety become dysfunctional, leading to excessive, persistent, and often inappropriate responses that significantly disrupt daily life and well-being. Unlike normal anxiety, which is adaptive and proportional to real threats, disordered anxiety is maladaptive and frequently disconnected from actual dangers. It is characterised by disproportionate intensity, prolonged duration, and impairment in daily functioning, including disruptions to relationships and mental health.

Defining the Forms of Disordered Anxiety

Anxiety manifests in different ways, each affecting people uniquely. Some common forms of disordered anxiety include:

Generalised Anxiety Disorder (GAD)

Generalised Anxiety Disorder is characterised by persistent, excessive worry about various aspects of daily life, such as health, work, relationships, or everyday events. People with GAD often find it difficult to control their worry, which leads to physical symptoms like fatigue, muscle tension, and difficulty sleeping. GAD can become a chronic condition, significantly affecting one's quality of life. Research by Barlow (2002) and Kessler (2005) highlights GAD as one of the most common forms of anxiety, affecting roughly 3-6% of the population. Barlow's work emphasises the underlying cognitive and emotional vulnerabilities that contribute to the persistence of anxiety.

Individuals with GAD may experience excessive worry about a range of issues, leading to chronic tension and stress. This maladaptive process can result in a cycle of worry that is disproportionate to the actual risks involved, impairing daily functioning.

Social Anxiety Disorder (SAD)

Social Anxiety Disorder involves intense fear or discomfort in social situations where one might be judged or scrutinised by others. This fear often leads to avoidance of social interactions, which can impair daily functioning, relationships, and work performance. Research by Clark and Wells (1995) highlights the role of distorted thinking patterns, such as fear of negative evaluation, in maintaining social anxiety. Their cognitive model of SAD has been foundational in understanding the development of avoidance behaviours and the intense self-focus that exacerbates symptoms.

The maladaptive processes in social anxiety involve intense fear of social situations and negative evaluation by others. This can lead to avoidance of social interactions, reinforcing feelings of isolation and anxiety over time.

Panic Disorder

Panic Disorder is marked by recurrent, unexpected panic attacks—sudden episodes of intense fear accompanied by physical symptoms such as a racing heart, shortness of breath, and dizziness. These attacks often lead to fear of future attacks, which can result in avoidance behaviours. Research by Craske and Barlow (2007) has identified the physiological and cognitive mechanisms that drive panic attacks, such as heightened sensitivity to bodily sensations and catastrophic misinterpretation of normal bodily functions.

In panic disorder, the maladaptive process often involves the misinterpretation of bodily sensations as signs of imminent danger (e.g., interpreting a racing heart as a heart attack). This can lead to avoidance behaviors and increased anxiety about experiencing future panic attacks.

Post-Traumatic Stress Disorder (PTSD)

PTSD is an anxiety disorder that develops after exposure to a traumatic event, such as violence, natural disasters, or accidents. Symptoms include flashbacks, nightmares, and severe anxiety, along with avoidance of stimuli related to the trauma. Research by Yehuda (2002) and van der Kolk (2014) shows how traumatic events can have lasting effects on the brain's fear circuitry, altering the way individuals respond to future stressors and contributing to emotional dysregulation.

The maladaptive process of Post-Traumatic Stress Disorder (PTSD) involves a complex interplay of mechanisms that perpetuate distress and impair functioning. Central to PTSD is hyperarousal, where heightened physiological responses, such as hypervigilance and an exaggerated startle reflex, keep individuals in a state of constant alertness, making it difficult to feel safe or relaxed. This heightened arousal is compounded by intrusive memories or flashbacks, which force individuals to relive the trauma repeatedly, often disrupting daily life. In response, avoidance behaviors develop as a way to minimise contact with trauma-related triggers. While avoidance may offer short-term relief, it reinforces the trauma, hinders emotional processing, and exacerbates isolation. Additionally, PTSD often involves negative alterations in cognition and mood, including persistent negative beliefs, feelings of detachment, and difficulty experiencing joy, all of which fuel hopelessness. Dysfunctional coping mechanisms, such as substance abuse, may arise as a way to manage overwhelming distress but ultimately intensify symptoms and create additional challenges. At its core, PTSD is marked by a failure to process and integrate the traumatic experience, leaving the trauma "frozen" in memory and perpetuating a cycle of chronic emotional and psychological suffering.

Obsessive-Compulsive Disorder (OCD)

OCD involves intrusive, unwanted thoughts (obsessions) that lead to repetitive behaviours (compulsions) aimed at reducing the anxiety caused by these thoughts. For example, an individual may engage in excessive hand-washing to neutralise fears of contamination. Research by Salkovskis (1985) and Abramowitz (2006) highlights the cognitive-behavioural processes behind OCD, emphasising how the misinterpretation of intrusive thoughts leads to compulsive rituals as a way to manage distress.

In OCD, maladaptive processes include the presence of intrusive thoughts (obsessions) that cause significant anxiety, leading to compulsive behaviors aimed at reducing that anxiety. These compulsions often provide only temporary relief and can interfere with daily life.

Forms of Maternal Anxiety

Some common forms of maternal anxiety include:

Prenatal Anxiety: Prenatal anxiety refers to the excessive worry or fear experienced by pregnant women about the health of their unborn child, the challenges of childbirth, or their ability to handle parenthood. Research by Glover (2014) and Dunkel Schetter (2011) shows that high levels of prenatal anxiety are linked to increased cortisol levels, which can affect fetal brain development and increase the risk of emotional and behavioural difficulties in children. These studies underscore the biological pathways through which maternal stress impacts the developing fetus.

Postpartum Anxiety: Postpartum anxiety occurs after childbirth and is often characterised by overwhelming worry about the baby's health, feeding, sleep, or safety. It can also involve physical symptoms such as heart palpitations, fatigue, and irritability. Mothers may reject their children after birth and are reluctant to feed or care for them is often associated with postpartum anxiety or postpartum depression. Mothers experiencing this form of anxiety may feel disconnected from their baby, fear they are inadequate caregivers, or worry excessively about doing something wrong. In more severe cases, this emotional distance can result in rejecting the baby or avoiding essential caregiving responsibilities. Research by Stuart and O'Hara (1995) highlights how postpartum anxiety differs from postpartum depression and emphasises the need for targeted interventions to reduce its impact on mother-infant bonding and maternal well-being. Stuart's work stresses the role of hormonal shifts and life adjustments that contribute to postpartum anxiety. Cheryl Tatano Beck, who has extensively studied postpartum mood disorders, and Diana Lynn Barnes, a leading expert on maternal mental health. Both have emphasised how untreated postpartum anxiety or depression can severely affect mother-child bonding and caregiving behaviors.

Separation Anxiety (in Mothers): Separation anxiety in mothers involves excessive fear or worry about being away from their child, especially in the early years. This can lead to overprotective behaviours and difficulty allowing the child independence. Bowlby's (1980) attachment theory suggests that maternal separation anxiety may stem from insecure attachment patterns formed during the mother's own early experiences. Subsequent research by Warren et al. (2003) supports the idea that maternal separation anxiety can influence how children develop their own attachment styles and emotional regulation.

Maternal Performance Anxiety: Maternal performance anxiety is characterised by the fear of not meeting societal or personal expectations of motherhood. This form of anxiety is often fuelled by external pressures, such as social media comparisons or cultural expectations of "perfect" parenting. Research by Leahy-Warren et al. (2012) highlights how modern societal pressures can exacerbate maternal anxiety, leading mothers to experience guilt, stress, and burnout. T

Maternal Health Anxiety (for the Child): Health anxiety in mothers is marked by excessive worry about their child's physical well-being, often leading to frequent medical checks, monitoring, and avoidance of activities perceived as risky. Research by Asmundson and Taylor (2005) suggests that maternal health anxiety can stem from cognitive distortions related to illness and injury, leading mothers to develop hypervigilant behaviours. This form of anxiety can affect both the mother's mental health and the child's sense of independence and confidence.

Each maternal anxiety type involves unique maladaptive processes that affect the mother's well-being and her ability to engage in healthy caregiving. Recognising and addressing these maladaptive patterns through therapeutic intervention, social support, and education is crucial to improving outcomes for both mother and child.

Conclusion

Each disorder has its unique characteristics, but they share common themes of excessive fear and avoidance that can lead to significant distress. Maternal anxiety is a significant mental health issue with far-reaching effects on mothers and their families. The emotional and psychological toll of untreated anxiety can lead to emotional dysregulation, strained relationships, and family instability.

Part two:

Conceptual Background

Chapter 4:

Human Vulnerability as Infants

———— ◦ ❋ ◦ ————

This chapter explores the profound helplessness of human infants, emphasising their early vulnerability and complete dependence on caregivers for survival. It underscores how this dependency plays a pivotal role in shaping their biological, cognitive, and emotional development.

Vulnerability of Infants

Human infants are among the most vulnerable newborns in the animal kingdom. Unlike many other mammals, such as deer or horses, which can walk or feed themselves shortly after birth, human infants are entirely dependent on their caregivers for survival. This extended period of vulnerability is due to a combination of biological, cognitive, and emotional factors that make human infancy a unique stage in mammalian development (Bjorklund & Pellegrini, 2002).

At birth, human babies lack the motor skills, sensory capacities, and strength to care for themselves. This is a stark contrast to other mammals, many of which have newborns that can move independently or feed themselves almost immediately after birth. For instance, deer and horses can walk within hours of being born, which allows them to flee from predators. This disparity arises because human infants are born with significantly underdeveloped bodies and brains, which leave them entirely reliant on caregivers for nourishment, protection, and warmth (Shonkoff & Phillips, 2000).

One key reason for this physical vulnerability is the relative size and development of the human brain at birth. While the brain is one of the largest organs relative to the rest of the body at birth, it is still only about 25% of its adult size. This necessitates an extended period of postnatal development (Giedd & Rapoport, 2010). In contrast, other mammals are born with brains that are closer to their adult size, allowing for more immediate motor skills and independence. The trade-off for humans is that the slower brain development allows for greater cognitive flexibility, emotional complexity, and social adaptability later in life.

Extended Period of Dependency

Human infants undergo one of the longest periods of dependency among mammals, known as the "childhood phase." This prolonged period of immaturity and reliance on caregivers allows infants to develop complex social and cognitive skills that are essential for navigating human societies (Konner, 2010). Unlike other species, where offspring develop basic survival skills quickly, human infants require years of learning and support to reach a stage where they can function independently.

This extended period of dependency has been shaped by evolutionary factors. It allows children to acquire essential skills like language, problem-solving, and social interaction, which are critical for survival in complex human environments. While other animals are born with more immediate physical abilities, humans benefit from this extended learning period, which promotes brain plasticity and adaptability (Bjorklund & Pellegrini, 2002). However, this developmental advantage comes at the cost of vulnerability, as human infants are entirely dependent on their caregivers for several years.

Sensory and Motor Skill Development

At birth, human sensory and motor systems are notably underdeveloped. Newborns have limited vision, weak motor control, and minimal muscle coordination, making them highly dependent on caregivers. In contrast, many animals are born with functional sensory systems and the ability to move, feed, and respond to threats. Human infants, however, take months or even years to develop full control over their motor functions and sensory processing (Shonkoff & Phillips, 2000).

The delayed development of sensory and motor skills in human infants is tied to the overall pace of brain maturation. The human brain grows rapidly during the first few years of life, but it takes time for neural circuits to mature and for sensory input to be integrated with motor actions. This gradual development allows for learning and adaptation, but it also leaves infants vulnerable during their early years (Giedd & Rapoport, 2010).

Brain Development and Cognitive Growth

Human brain development is characterised by remarkable plasticity during the early years of life, which allows infants to learn and adapt to their environment. At birth, the brain is about 25% of its adult size but grows rapidly, reaching approximately 80% of adult size by age two. However, it takes several more years for the brain's neural networks to become fully functional and integrated (Shonkoff & Phillips, 2000).

This slow brain maturation is both an advantage and a vulnerability. On one hand, it means that infants are highly dependent on caregivers for an extended period. On the other hand, it allows for a high degree of learning and adaptability, particularly in areas like language development, social interaction, and emotional regulation. The delayed maturation of the human brain is a critical factor in the extended childhood phase, allowing children to develop complex cognitive and social skills that are essential for later life success (Giedd & Rapoport, 2010).

Emotional and Social Vulnerability

Beyond physical and cognitive vulnerabilities, human infants are also emotionally and socially dependent on their caregivers. John Bowlby's attachment theory underscores the importance of early bonding between infants and caregivers, typically the mother, for healthy emotional development (Bowlby, 1988). Secure attachment provides the infant with a sense of safety and security, allowing them to explore the world with confidence.

This emotional dependency sets humans apart from many other species. While animal offspring may rely on their parents for food and protection, human infants require emotional and social guidance to develop the skills needed to navigate complex social structures. The extended period of dependency allows for the development of these skills, which are vital for long-term survival and success in human societies (Konner, 2010).

Susceptibility to Anxiety Issues

When caregivers are attuned to an infant's needs, they help regulate the infant's stress responses, promoting a sense of safety and stability. However, inconsistent or neglectful caregiving can disrupt this process, increasing the infant's susceptibility to anxiety.

Biologically, the infant's underdeveloped nervous system amplifies their sensitivity to environmental cues, including caregiver stress. Research by Meaney (2001) highlights how early-life stress can dysregulate the hypothalamic-pituitary-adrenal (HPA) axis, a key system involved in stress responses, predisposing the infant to heightened anxiety. Maternal anxiety, for example, can influence the intrauterine environment through elevated cortisol levels, which affect fetal brain development. Postnatally, an anxious caregiver's hypervigilance or overprotection may inadvertently reinforce the infant's perception of the world as unsafe, contributing to long-term anxiety risks.

Furthermore, early experiences of unpredictability or trauma can imprint deeply on the developing brain. Neural plasticity, while beneficial for adaptation, also means that negative experiences during infancy can have lasting effects on emotional and physiological regulation. Studies by Evans et al. (2008) indicate that infants exposed to chronic stress or inconsistent caregiving are more likely to develop heightened stress sensitivity, emotional dysregulation, and anxiety disorders in later childhood and adulthood.

Infants are remarkably sensitive to the emotional states of their caregivers, a trait deeply rooted in their evolutionary need for survival. This sensitivity allows infants to pick up on cues of anxiety, stress, or emotional instability in their caregivers, which can imprint onto their developing memories and shape their emotional and physiological responses.

Conclusion

Human infants are born with a unique set of vulnerabilities that make them highly dependent on caregivers for survival. These vulnerabilities arise from a combination of physical, cognitive, and emotional immaturity, tied to the slow development of the human brain and body. Unlike many mammals that exhibit greater physical independence at birth, human infants require prolonged care and support to acquire the skills necessary for thriving in complex social environments. During this critical period of dependency, any anxiety experienced or expressed by caregivers can profoundly shape an infant's emotional framework.

Chapter 5:

Anxiety as Genetic Formation

───── ◌ ⚶ ◌ ─────

Is anxiety inherited through genetic factors, or is it a learned behavior shaped by family dynamics and environmental influences, particularly during early childhood? This chapter, along with the next, delves into the complexities of the nature vs. nurture debate. It also explores the emerging field of epigenetics and highlights the powerful role environmental and social factors play in shaping a child's predisposition to anxiety. By examining the interplay between genetic and environmental elements, these chapters provide valuable insights into how anxiety develops and how it can be mitigated through targeted interventions and supportive environments.

The Genetic Basis of Anxiety

Research estimates that 30-50% of the variability in anxiety traits is heritable, demonstrating the strong role of genetic factors. These genetic predispositions influence the functioning of key neurotransmitters such as serotonin, dopamine, and GABA, which are critical for mood regulation, stress responses, and emotional stability. For instance, the 5-HTTLPR gene, associated with serotonin regulation, has been linked to increased anxiety levels. Similarly, genes involved in the hypothalamic-pituitary-adrenal (HPA) axis, responsible for managing the body's stress response, play a vital role in determining susceptibility to anxiety disorders. Twin studies have consistently shown that conditions like generalised anxiety disorder (GAD), panic disorder, and social anxiety disorder often run in families, further supporting the genetic basis of anxiety.

A landmark genome-wide association study (GWAS) led by Renato Polimanti in 2024 analysed data from over 1.2 million participants and identified more than 100 genes associated with anxiety disorders. This study emphasised the importance of genes expressed in the limbic system and cerebral cortex, regions essential for regulating emotions. These findings underscore the need to integrate data from diverse populations and use multi-omic approaches to better understand the genetic factors contributing to anxiety. Complementary research, such as Stein et al. (2018), highlights the importance of genetic risk during critical developmental periods like childhood and adolescence, suggesting targeted opportunities for intervention.

Genetic Studies and Neurobiology

Genetic studies, such as those by Hettema et al. (2001), highlight the heritability of anxiety disorders, showing how inherited traits shape neural mechanisms involved in fear and stress regulation. This underscores the vulnerability of individuals with a family history of anxiety to these disorders and emphasises the potential for personalised treatments tailored to genetic profiles. Gregory and Eley (2007) further explored how genetic predispositions influence brain functions like emotional regulation and threat perception, emphasising the interplay between genetic factors and environmental triggers, such as parenting styles and early stressors, in exacerbating anxiety vulnerabilities. Smoller et al. (2009) identified key genetic markers, like variants in the serotonin transporter gene (SLC6A4), linking neurotransmitter regulation to anxiety and supporting targeted pharmacological interventions for these neurochemical imbalances.

Gene-Environment and Anxiety Development

While genetics play a foundational role, the interaction between genetic predispositions and environmental factors significantly influences the manifestation of anxiety disorders. Pine and Fox (2015) explored how genetic vulnerabilities interact with early environmental stressors, such as parental anxiety or childhood trauma, to shape neurobiological systems responsible for emotional regulation. Sensitive periods in childhood amplify the effects of these genetic-environment interactions, often leading to persistent anxiety into adulthood.

Stein and Smoller (2018) provide an integrative perspective on the shared and distinct genetic pathways influencing anxiety and related conditions like depression. Their work emphasises how genetic susceptibility can alter stress and fear processing in the brain, offering insights into precision medicine approaches.

Temperament and Genetic Predisposition

The interplay between genetic predisposition and temperament is another critical factor in understanding anxiety. Jerome Kagan's (1988) research on behavioural inhibition highlights how some children are genetically predisposed to high emotional reactivity, exhibiting traits such as fearfulness, shyness, or nervousness. These temperament traits, reflecting heightened sensitivity in the stress-response system, indicate an inherited vulnerability to anxiety disorders. Kagan's studies reveal that infants who strongly react to unfamiliar stimuli are more likely to develop social or generalised anxiety disorders later in life.

Joseph LeDoux's (2000) research on the amygdala further supports this perspective by examining its role in fear processing. His work demonstrates how early exposure to fearful events or anxious environments can condition children to develop long-term anxiety. These findings underscore the importance of environmental influences in shaping the expression of genetic predispositions, illustrating how inherited traits interact with life experiences to manifest as anxiety.

Genetic Susceptibility

Genetic susceptibility to anxiety is strongly linked to familial history, influencing brain chemistry, fear processing, and the body's alarm system, making individuals more vulnerable to stress dysregulation. Hettema et al. (2001) demonstrated significant heritability in anxiety disorders, tying genetic factors to neural mechanisms involved in fear and stress regulation. Gregory and Eley (2007) emphasised the transmission of anxiety traits within families, highlighting alterations in brain function related to emotional regulation and threat perception.

Smoller et al. (2009) identified genetic markers, such as SLC6A4 variants, linking neurotransmitter systems to anxiety, while Pine and Fox (2015) explored how genetic predispositions interact with early environmental stressors, shaping neurobiological systems. Stein and Smoller (2018) expanded on these findings, showing shared genetic pathways between anxiety and depression, further elucidating the interplay between inherited traits and environmental influences in the development of anxiety disorders.

Interaction Between Genetics and Environment

David Reiss's research highlights the complex interplay between inherited traits and family environments, demonstrating that genetics alone does not dictate the development of anxiety. For instance, a child with a genetic tendency toward anxiety may not develop a full-blown disorder unless raised in a high-stress environment characterised by parental conflict, emotional neglect, or chronic exposure to maternal anxiety. Conversely, a supportive and low-stress environment can mitigate these genetic risks, underscoring the powerful role of environmental factors in amplifying or reducing susceptibility to anxiety.

Epigenetics and Environmental Influence

Epigenetics provides further insights into how environmental factors influence gene expression, adding complexity to the nature vs. nurture debate. Epigenetic mechanisms act as switches that turn specific genes on or off in response to environmental stimuli. In the context of anxiety, while a genetic predisposition may exist, environmental influences such as maternal stress, trauma, or chronic anxiety can determine whether these genes are activated.

Research by Rachel Yehuda (2002) on trauma and epigenetics highlights the transgenerational impact of environmental stressors. Her studies on the descendants of Holocaust survivors revealed that traumatic experiences in parents can lead to epigenetic changes, predisposing their children to anxiety and emotional dysregulation. Similarly, maternal stress during pregnancy elevates cortisol levels that cross the placenta, impacting fetal brain development and altering the child's stress-regulation system.

Conclusion

The genetic basis of anxiety is a critical area of research that sheds light on the complex interplay between inherited traits and environmental influences. Genetic predispositions, particularly those affecting neurotransmitter systems and stress-regulation pathways, play a foundational role in determining vulnerability to anxiety disorders.

Chapter 6:

Anxiety as Learned Behaviour

Anxiety is a multifaceted condition influenced not only by genetic predispositions but also by learned behaviors and environmental factors. While genetic inheritance provides a biological foundation for susceptibility, learned anxiety arises from observation, social modelling, and life experiences, emphasising the critical role of nurture. Understanding how anxiety can be learned helps unravel its complexities, providing pathways for effective prevention and intervention strategies.

Learned Helplessness and Anxiety Transmission

Martin Seligman's foundational research (1972) on learned helplessness sheds light on the development of anxiety through uncontrollable stress. In his experiments, rats subjected to unavoidable stress eventually stopped attempting to escape, even when escape became possible. This state of emotional paralysis mirrors human anxiety and depression, where individuals feel powerless to influence their circumstances.

In familial contexts, children exposed to parental and maternal anxiety in particular may internalise this sense of helplessness. When a parent consistently reacts to challenges with heightened anxiety or resignation, his or her children may mirror these responses, learning to perceive their environment as uncontrollable and threatening. This learned helplessness becomes ingrained, shaping the child's worldview and increasing their susceptibility to anxiety disorders later in life.

Modelling and Mirroring of Anxiety

Albert Bandura's social learning theory (1977, 2001) underscores the role of observation in shaping behavior. According to Bandura, individuals, especially children, learn by observing and imitating the behaviors of others. For children, parents—particularly mothers—serve as primary role models in navigating emotional and social challenges. When parents display anxious behaviors, such as avoidance, over-worrying, or exaggerated fear responses, children often adopt these reactions as their own. For instance, a child observing a parent's intense fear during thunderstorms might develop a similar phobia, even without experiencing a traumatic event themselves. Anxiety can also be transmitted within peer groups. Observing classmates react with fear or stress to academic pressures can lead to the internalisation of similar emotional patterns. Mineka and Cook (1988) demonstrated that primates could learn fear responses to snakes simply by observing other primates exhibiting fear, even without any direct negative experiences. This finding parallels how children adopt anxious behaviors from caregivers or peers.

Emotional Contagion: The Subtle Spread of Anxiety

Emotional contagion is the unconscious mirroring of another's emotional state. It plays a critical role in how anxiety is transmitted within close relationships, particularly between parents and children. This process involves non-verbal cues, such as facial expressions, tone of voice, and body language, which children naturally attune to, especially in their primary caregivers.

A mother's anxious demeanour can subtly convey a sense of danger, prompting the child to adopt similar emotional responses. For instance, if a mother reacts with visible fear to minor mishaps, her child may internalise this response, developing a heightened sensitivity to stress. Over time, the child's consistent exposure to anxious cues reinforces their perception of the world as unsafe, contributing to a chronic state of hyper-vigilance. Elaine Hatfield's work on emotional contagion illustrates how anxiety spreads within intimate relationships. Her studies confirm that children are especially vulnerable to absorbing and internalising their parents' emotional states, which profoundly influences their emotional development.

Conditioning Processes: Classical and Operant

Classical Conditioning: Classical conditioning involves associating a neutral stimulus with an anxiety-inducing event, leading to a conditioned fear response. This mechanism is often responsible for developing specific phobias. A child bitten by a dog may begin to fear all dogs, associating them with pain and danger. A student embarrassed during a classroom presentation may develop a fear of public speaking, avoiding similar situations in the future. Over time, these associations persist even without the original triggering event, demonstrating how anxiety can develop independently of genetic factors.

Operant Conditioning: Operant conditioning reinforces behaviors through rewards or consequences, inadvertently perpetuating anxiety. Avoidance as Reinforcement: Avoiding anxiety-inducing situations provides immediate relief, reinforcing the behavior. For example, a child who skips school to avoid bullying experiences temporary comfort, solidifying the belief that avoidance is the best coping strategy. Long-Term Effects: This avoidance inhibits exposure to and desensitisation from feared stimuli, exacerbating anxiety over time. Anxiety can also be learned through verbal communication, where caregivers or authority figures emphasise risks and dangers, often unintentionally instilling fear. Overemphasis on Threats: Constant warnings about potential dangers (e.g., "Don't talk to strangers; they're dangerous!") can create a heightened sense of fear in children, even in safe situations. Adults who frequently describe worst-case scenarios may foster hyper-vigilance and exaggerated anxiety in children. For example, a parent who repeatedly warns a child about the dangers of climbing trees might inadvertently discourage exploration and install a generalised fear of physical activity.

Environmental Reinforcement and Chronic Stress

Certain environments can foster the development of anxiety, particularly those marked by unpredictability, conflict, or neglect. Growing up in a household with frequent parental conflict or instability teaches children that their world is unsafe, leading to generalised anxiety. In addition, exposure to trauma or neglect disrupts emotional regulation and fosters hyper-vigilance as an adaptive survival mechanism. Further, children who do not receive validation or comfort from caregivers may struggle to develop healthy coping mechanisms, making them more vulnerable to anxiety. Kitzmann et al. (2003) found that children exposed to high-conflict environments exhibited significantly higher rates of anxiety and emotional dysregulation than those in stable households.

The Feedback Loop: Reinforcing Anxious Behaviors

Anxiety can become entrenched through a feedback loop where anxious behaviors in parents and children reinforce one another. For example, a mother who is overly protective may constantly warn her child about potential dangers, prompting the child to adopt a hyper-vigilant approach to their surroundings. The child's heightened fear responses, in turn, validate the mother's anxiety, perpetuating the cycle. This dynamic creates a self-sustaining pattern where both parent and child reinforce each other's fears.

Conclusion

Understanding the mechanisms of learned anxiety offers critical insights into breaking the cycle and fostering healthier emotional development. Learned anxiety emphasises the role of environmental and experiential factors in shaping emotional responses. While genetic predispositions play a role, anxiety is often reinforced through social modelling, verbal transmission, and conditioning processes.

Chapter 7:

Anxiety From an Evolutionary Perspective

This chapter intends to elaborate the evolutionary psychology perspective of anxiety as it is the main approach of our research. By applying evolutionary psychology theories, we can analyse the factors that contribute to anxiety's maladaptive manifestations and its persistence across populations.

Mismatch Theory in Anxiety

Mismatch theory explains how traits that evolved under ancestral conditions become maladaptive in modern environments due to rapid societal changes. Anxiety, essential for survival in dangerous contexts, relied on a "better safe than sorry" approach to detect and respond to threats. Tooby and Cosmides (1990) highlighted its role in avoiding predators and conflicts, while Nesse and Williams (1994) framed it through the "smoke detector principle," prioritising survival over false alarms. However, in modern settings with fewer immediate dangers, these mechanisms can lead to chronic worry and disorders like generalised anxiety disorder (GAD).

Modern social structures amplify mismatches in anxiety's functionality. Humans evolved in small groups where social rejection threatened survival, making social anxiety crucial for cohesion. Baumeister and Leary (1995) observed that today's large, fluid social networks hyperactivate these mechanisms, leading to excessive fear of evaluation or rejection in contexts like public speaking. Environmental mismatches also reveal anxiety's miscalibration; Seligman's (1971) "preparedness theory" shows that while humans easily fear ancestral threats like snakes, modern stressors—financial instability or online harassment—trigger maladaptive responses, as Öhman and Mineka (2001) found.

Parenting and childhood contexts further underscore mismatched conditions. Overprotective parenting in safe environments deprives children of resilience, as Ellis et al. (2011) noted, while Twenge (2000) highlighted academic pressures and reduced play as anxiety triggers. Urbanisation, noise pollution, and sedentary lifestyles exacerbate modern stress, correlating with heightened anxiety and cognitive impairment, as Evans and Lepore (1993) and Hansen et al. (2001) demonstrated. These mismatches reveal how ancestral mechanisms, though once adaptive, can misfire in contemporary settings.

Smoke Detector Principle

The smoke detector principle, introduced by Nesse and Williams (1994), explains the evolutionary rationale behind the design of anxiety systems that prioritise caution over precision. Anxiety is likened to a smoke detector, which is better programmed to produce frequent false alarms than to miss a real fire. This approach is grounded in the evolutionary trade-off between the costs of false positives (unnecessary anxiety) and false negatives (failing to detect a real threat). In ancestral environments, missing a life-threatening danger could lead to death, making a cautious response mechanism critical for survival, even if it sometimes resulted in unnecessary fear or worry.

Key aspects of the principle include error management and the threshold for activation. Anxiety mechanisms are designed to favour survival by triggering responses to ambiguous or low-level threats. This low activation threshold ensured early humans could respond to potential dangers like predators or intergroup conflicts, even when the threat was uncertain. However, in modern environments, where immediate life-threatening dangers are rare, this same low threshold often leads to overactivation of anxiety systems. This mismatch contributes to the prevalence of anxiety disorders such as generalised anxiety disorder (GAD), which reflect miscalibrations of what were once adaptive systems.

Empirical evidence supports this principle and its implications. Nesse (2005) highlighted that anxiety disorders are not defects but represent the evolutionary cost of avoiding catastrophic outcomes. Similarly, Öhman and Mineka (2001) found that humans and animals are more predisposed to develop anxiety for evolutionarily relevant threats (e.g., snakes, spiders) than modern ones, emphasising the principle's survival focus.

Costly Signalling Theory

Costly signalling theory, from evolutionary biology, explains how organisms send reliable signals by incurring significant costs. In psychology, it suggests that anxiety may serve as a costly signal of reliability, commitment, or social awareness. Behaviors like heightened vigilance or concern for others demonstrate attunement to group welfare, with their emotional and energetic costs ensuring authenticity.

Empirical evidence supports this concept. Zahavi and Zahavi (1997) highlighted the reliability of costly signals in animals, a principle extended to human anxiety by Gilbert (2001). In modern contexts, moderate anxiety can signal diligence and responsibility, benefiting professional and social outcomes, while excessive anxiety risks undermining these advantages.

Life History Theory

Life history theory explains how organisms allocate limited resources to growth, reproduction, and survival. Anxiety aligns with fast and slow life history strategies shaped by environmental conditions. In high-risk, unpredictable environments, fast strategies prioritise immediate survival and reproduction, with anxiety manifesting as vigilance and quick decision-making. In stable environments, slow strategies focus on long-term planning and parental care, where anxiety promotes caution and strategic risk management.

Research supports these ideas. Ellis et al. (2009) linked unstable environments to higher anxiety and impulsivity, reflecting fast strategies. Del Giudice (2014) noted that anxiety disorders often emerge when strategies mismatch environmental risks, such as chronic anxiety from fast strategies in stable settings or excessive caution from slow strategies in uncertain conditions.

Reproductive behaviors also reflect these strategies. Fast strategies, driven by anxiety, may prioritise early reproduction but limit offspring due to resource constraints. Slow strategies with high parental investment can foster overprotectiveness, perpetuating anxiety across generations.

Neurobiological and Cognitive Mechanisms

Prepared Learning

Prepared learning is an evolutionary adaptation enabling humans to quickly associate certain stimuli, such as predators or heights, with danger. This mechanism evolved to ensure survival in ancestral environments, where recognising threats like snakes or spiders could prevent fatal encounters. These associations are formed rapidly, resistant to extinction, and common even in individuals without direct exposure, highlighting their evolutionary significance.

The brain's fear-processing systems, particularly the amygdala, drive prepared learning by forming rapid and lasting fear associations. The amygdala's connection to the hippocampus reinforces these memories, enabling individuals to avoid similar threats in the future. While adaptive in ancestral settings, these mechanisms can become maladaptive in safe modern environments.

Research supports prepared learning as an ingrained survival strategy. Mineka and Öhman (2002) found humans and primates more easily fear evolutionarily relevant stimuli, like snakes, than neutral ones. Similarly, Cook and Mineka (1989) demonstrated that monkeys quickly learn fear of snakes through observation, but not neutral objects. The universality of such fears across cultures underscores their deep evolutionary roots.

Overgeneralisation

Overgeneralisation occurs when fear responses extend beyond actual threats, resulting in maladaptive outcomes. While prepared learning helps individuals associate real dangers with fear, overgeneralisation leads to irrational fears of benign stimuli. For example, a person bitten by a dog might develop an undue fear of all dogs, even harmless ones. This process underpins many anxiety disorders, such as phobias and generalised anxiety disorder (GAD).

Cognitive and neurobiological factors contribute to overgeneralisation. Memory encoding errors and cognitive biases cause anxious individuals to interpret ambiguous stimuli as threatening. An overactive amygdala amplifies fear, while an impaired prefrontal cortex fails to regulate it effectively, perpetuating fear responses even in safe environments.

Research underscores the role of overgeneralisation in anxiety. Lissek et al. (2010) showed that individuals with anxiety disorders fear a wider range of stimuli, and Grillon (2002) found they struggle to extinguish fear after the original threat is gone. This maladaptive extension of fear disrupts functioning and transforms adaptive survival mechanisms into chronic anxiety.

Social Implications of Anxiety

Anxiety plays a critical role in maintaining social cohesion, promoting behaviors that align with group norms and discourage conflict. In ancestral environments, anxiety helped individuals avoid actions that could lead to exclusion or resource loss, ensuring group harmony and access to collective benefits. Even today, moderate social anxiety promotes positive traits such as politeness, vigilance, and empathy, enhancing trust and cooperation in structured environments. However, when anxiety becomes excessive, as in social anxiety disorder (SAD), it can lead to avoidance of social interactions, negative self-perception, and chronic loneliness, undermining its adaptive purpose.

Empirical evidence supports anxiety's evolutionary function in social dynamics. Baumeister and Leary (1995) described social anxiety as part of the "need to belong," incentivising behaviors that maintain group membership. Leary and Kowalski (1995) highlighted that while moderate anxiety enhances social functioning by fostering cooperation and conflict avoidance, excessive anxiety reduces social effectiveness and increases isolation. In hierarchical contexts, anxiety about preserving status can drive conscientiousness and improved performance. However, excessive workplace anxiety may impair decision-making and productivity, revealing the fine line between adaptive and maladaptive anxiety.

Reproductive Implications of Anxiety

Anxiety shapes reproductive strategies by promoting caution in mate selection and protective parenting, which were adaptive in ancestral environments to enhance offspring survival. However, in modern low-risk contexts, excessive anxiety can disrupt hormonal balance, strain relationships, and lead to overprotective parenting, fostering dependence and perpetuating anxiety across generations.

Although once beneficial in high-risk settings, anxious parenting in safer environments can hinder children's resilience and autonomy. Intergenerational cycles of anxiety arise through genetic predispositions and anxious behaviors, posing challenges to mental health and family dynamics today.

Chronic anxiety also impacts fertility and reproductive timing. Stress-induced hormonal imbalances disrupt ovulation and sperm quality, while anxiety aligns with early reproduction in unstable environments. In contrast, stable contexts favour delayed reproduction and greater parental investment. These maladaptive expressions of anxiety in modern settings can strain relationships and reduce reproductive fitness.

Evolutionary fitness of anxiety

Anxiety evolved as an adaptive mechanism, enhancing survival through vigilance, threat detection, and protective behaviors. In ancestral environments, it fostered group cohesion and cautious parenting, improving reproductive success and offspring survival. However, in modern contexts with fewer physical threats, anxiety often misfires, leading to maladaptive outcomes.

In contemporary settings, novel stressors like financial pressures and social evaluation chronically activate stress responses, contributing to health issues like cardiovascular disease and depression. Socially, anxiety heightens fears of rejection, hindering relationships and career growth. Overprotective parenting, once beneficial, now limits children's independence, perpetuating maladaptive anxiety cycles.

Anxiety represents an evolutionary trade-off, offering survival benefits but imposing costs when excessive. Moderate anxiety promotes vigilance and cohesion, but extreme forms impair health and productivity. Addressing its modern misalignment is essential to reduce dysfunction while preserving its adaptive value.

Conclusion

Anxiety's maladaptive nature in modern environments reflects the interplay of evolutionary trade-offs, environmental mismatch, and imperfect regulatory systems. By analysing anxiety through the lens of evolutionary psychology, we can better understand its origins, persistence, and impact. This perspective not only clarifies the mechanisms underlying anxiety disorders but also highlights opportunities for more effective, evolution-informed prevention and treatment strategies.

Chapter 8:

How We Perceive Evolutionary Threats

―――― ❧ ――――

This chapter explores the perceived evolutionary threats that commonly surface among clients experiencing anxiety in therapeutic environments.

Perceived Threats and the Amygdala

The amygdala, the brain's central hub for emotional processing, is designed to detect threats and initiate survival responses. It plays a critical role in interpreting perceived threats, which often arise from unmet psychological and emotional needs. These needs are fundamental to human well-being, and when compromised, the amygdala triggers reactions that can manifest as anxiety, fear, and defensive behaviors. In therapeutic settings, such perceived threats frequently emerge through clients' narratives and repeated language patterns, offering insights into their underlying emotional struggles.

Narratives and Repeated Language Patterns

Narratives and repeated language patterns in clients with severe anxiety often act as internal "programs" that perpetuate their anxious responses. Shaped by deep fears, cognitive distortions, and unmet emotional needs, these patterns repeatedly activate the brain's threat detection system, particularly the amygdala. Phrases like "What if something goes wrong?" or "I can't handle this" create a feedback loop of perceived threats, reinforcing a sense of helplessness and triggering physiological and emotional responses such as stress, avoidance, and hypervigilance.

These mental scripts filter experiences through fear and inadequacy, sustaining anxiety. For instance, social anxiety narratives like "Everyone is judging me" lead to avoidance, preventing disconfirmation of fears, while catastrophic thoughts like "Something terrible will happen" reinforce a belief in a dangerous world. Breaking these cycles involves identifying and challenging such narratives, enabling clients to adopt more realistic and calming thought patterns.

Modern Perceived Threats and Narratives

According to Choice Theory, developed by William Glasser, all behavior is purposeful and motivated by the drive to fulfill basic needs in an adaptive manner. At any given moment, our actions reflect our best effort to achieve what we desire based on the information available to us. Glasser identified these basic needs as encompassing both physical and psychological elements. While physical needs like survival are fundamental, psychological needs—categorised as love and belonging,

66

power, freedom, and fun—are equally vital for overall well-being. Unmet psychological needs often result in the perception of threats, contributing to emotional and behavioural challenges.

Building on Choice Theory, this chapter identifies three primary perceived threats in the modern world: security, love and belonging, and success (self-esteem needs). It examines how the amygdala responds to these threats and highlights the recurring narratives in which they surface in therapeutic contexts.

Perceived Threats to Security

The need for security is deeply rooted in survival instincts. Security encompasses both physical safety and emotional stability, including feeling safe in relationships, environments, and life circumstances. When this need is threatened, the amygdala responds as though the individual's survival is at risk, initiating the fight-or-flight response.

Narratives of Security Threats: "My life is in danger." "I am insecure." "I am going to die" "I am vulnerable to harm."

These perceived threats could be triggered by anything from real physical danger to more abstract fears, such as job instability, relationship uncertainty, or fear of future outcomes. The amygdala's quick response mechanism bypasses rational thinking and floods the body with stress hormones like cortisol and adrenaline.

Amygdala's Reaction:

Fight-or-flight response: The body becomes hypervigilant, preparing to escape or confront the perceived threat. Symptoms include increased heart rate, rapid breathing, and muscle tension.

Emotional outcome: Anxiety and fear are the dominant emotions that emerge as the amygdala gears the body up for survival.

Physical sensations: Trembling, sweating, dizziness, and nausea.

Behavioural Response: Individuals might engage in avoidance, defensiveness, or over-control as a way to regain a sense of security. Avoidance might manifest as procrastination in addressing stressful situations, while defensiveness could be expressed as anger or irritability when feeling threatened.

Perceived Threats to Love and Belonging

The need for love and belonging is another fundamental human necessity. It reflects the desire to form close relationships, to be accepted, and to feel valued within social groups. Threats to this need often centre around feelings of rejection, abandonment, or social exclusion.

Narrative of Threats: "I have not been loved." "I have not been accepted." "I have not been approved". "I do not belong."

When individuals feel unloved, not accepted or excluded, the amygdala interprets these experiences as threats to their social survival, group survival rooted in evolutionary mechanisms. In early human history, social exclusion could mean isolation from the group, which posed real dangers to survival.

Amygdala's Reaction:

Fear of rejection: The amygdala triggers anxiety and sadness, reinforcing the need to either restore connection or withdraw to protect against further emotional pain.

Emotional outcome: Shame, guilt, loneliness, and emptiness are common emotional reactions when the need for belonging is threatened.

Physical sensations: Individuals may experience stomach discomfort (the sensation of "butterflies"), headaches, fatigue, or chest tightness.

Behavioural Response: Individuals may engage in people-pleasing, overcompensating behaviours, or withdrawal. Defensive behaviours may also arise, such as blaming others or becoming overly critical, as a way to guard against the perceived threat of rejection. In some cases, they may demand constant reassurance or become clingy in relationships to restore a sense of belonging.

Perceived Threats to Success and Control

The need for success, control, and power is closely related to one's sense of competence and autonomy. Success involves achievement in personal and professional life, while control refers to the ability to influence one's circumstances. When these needs are threatened, it can lead to feelings of inadequacy, failure, and helplessness.

Narrative of Threats: "I have no control." "I am not good enough." "I am a failure."

These threats trigger a fear of being powerless or unsuccessful, which can damage self-esteem. The amygdala, interpreting this as a critical threat, activates stress responses that prepare the individual to either regain control or withdraw from the challenge.

Amygdala's Reaction:

Fear of failure: The amygdala generates anxiety and frustration, as it prepares the body for action but also leaves the individual vulnerable to feelings of defeat.

Emotional outcome: Helplessness, anger, shame, and guilt often arise when individuals feel that they lack power or control over important areas of their life.

Physical sensations: Increased muscle tension, headaches, and fatigue are common as the individual faces mounting pressure to succeed or regain control.

Behavioural Response: Common survival strategies include avoidance, procrastination, and overworking in an attempt to achieve perfection or regain a sense of control. Some individuals may also engage in defensiveness or justification, refusing to acknowledge mistakes or failures to protect their sense of self-worth.

The amygdala, in its role as the brain's threat detector, triggers a cycle where perceived threats activate emotions and bodily responses, which then influence behaviours. These behaviours often lead to negative consequences, such as social rejection or failure to meet goals, reinforcing the initial perceived threats.

Recovery from perceived threat

The fight-or-flight response initiated by the amygdala is a temporary but essential reaction to perceived threats. When the brain detects a danger, the amygdala signals the release of stress hormones like adrenaline, preparing the body for immediate action—either to confront the threat (fight) or to escape it (flight). This reaction is intended to be short-lived, allowing the body to respond quickly to immediate dangers.

However, the amygdala also has a regaining and recovery function. Once the threat is gone, other parts of the brain, particularly the prefrontal cortex, help regulate the amygdala's response, signalling the body to return to a calm state. This allows the nervous system to recover from the heightened alertness of the fight-or-flight response, restoring balance and preventing chronic stress. This recovery mechanism is vital for maintaining emotional and physiological health, preventing prolonged anxiety that can become harmful when triggered too often or unnecessarily in modern environments.

Conclusion

The amygdala plays a crucial role in triggering emotional and physiological responses when fundamental human needs—such as security, love and belonging, or success—are threatened or perceived as threatened. These perceived threats can activate a cascade of emotional reactions and physical sensations that influence behavior and decision-making. The real issue arises when perceived threats become excessive or long-standing, leading to chronic stress or anxiety. Fortunately, the brain has a natural recovery process that helps regulate these responses. By understanding these patterns, individuals can disrupt maladaptive reactions and develop healthier coping strategies, enabling them to manage perceived threats more effectively and regain emotional balance.

Part Three:

Behavioural Display and Transmission

Chapter 9:

Behavioural Display of Anxiety

⊙ ⚬ ⚘ ⚬ ⊙

This chapter examines anxiety-related behaviors and personality traits in individuals, as observed in therapeutic settings. It discusses how these behaviors, when exhibited by parents, influence family relationships, notably affecting children's emotional and social development.

Temperament and Behavioural Inhibition

An anxious parents' temperament profoundly affects their children's emotional landscape. Children of anxious parents often develop a reactive temperament, characterised by heightened sensitivity and behavioural inhibition. This manifests as shyness, withdrawal, and fear in new social situations (Kagan et al., 2003). These children may find it difficult to form friendships or engage in group activities due to their tendency to avoid social interactions. An anxious parents' overprotective behaviors, often rooted in their anxiety, can reinforce these tendencies, creating a feedback loop that strengthens anxiety in both parent and child. The child's withdrawal increases the parents' concerns, which may lead parents to be even more protective, perpetuating the cycle of anxiety.

Low Tolerance for Uncertainty

Many anxious parents display a low tolerance for uncertainty, resulting in rigid routines and a need to control situations. This behavior is easily absorbed by children, leading them to develop their own anxieties about unpredictability. According to Dugas and Ladouceur (2000), intolerance of uncertainty is a core feature of anxiety disorders. In a family context, this behavior can manifest in excessive worry about minor uncertainties, such as changes in daily routines or external events like bad weather. Children raised in such environments may struggle to cope with new situations, limiting their emotional flexibility and ability to adapt to life's challenges. This rigidity can lead to conflict as children grow older and seek more independence, which often clashes with the parent's need for control.

Hypervigilance and Agitation

Hypervigilance, a state of heightened alertness often seen in anxious parents, leads to increased agitation and overreaction to perceived threats. This behavior creates an environment where children internalise their parents' constant worry, becoming overly cautious and fearful themselves (Barrett & Turner, 2001). The heightened tension resulting from the parents' hypervigilance can disrupt family dynamics, creating an atmosphere of stress and anxiety that affects all members. Children may learn to mirror their parents' anxious behavior, further perpetuating a cycle of fear within the household. Communication in such families often breaks down, as emotional exchanges are dominated by the need to manage perceived threats rather than engage in constructive dialogue.

Perfectionism and Fear of Failure

Anxious parents frequently impose perfectionistic tendencies on themselves and their children. The fear of failure— whether academic, social, or personal—transfers to children, who may feel immense pressure to meet their parents' expectations. Flett et al. (2002) note that parental perfectionism is linked to increased anxiety in children, who struggle to meet unrealistic standards. This pressure can manifest in avoidance behaviors, procrastination, or burnout, as children become overwhelmed by the fear of not meeting expectations. These behaviors strain family relationships, as the child's internalised anxiety often results in emotional outbursts, further perpetuating feelings of inadequacy and fear of failure.

Emotional Reactivity and Sensitivity

Parents with anxiety often exhibit heightened emotional reactivity, which has a profound impact on their children's emotional development. Anxious parents may overreact to stress, creating an emotionally charged environment where children learn to be hyper-attuned to their parents' moods (Morris et al., 2007). This heightened sensitivity can lead to emotional dysregulation in children, who may become volatile or withdrawn when faced with stress. The emotionally reactive environment creates frequent conflict within the family, as both the anxious parents and their children struggle to regulate their emotions effectively, leading to breakdowns in communication and emotional connection.

Inability to Draw Boundaries

Anxious parents who struggle to set boundaries often find it difficult to say "no" and may agree to requests or demands even when they feel overwhelmed or uncomfortable. This behavior often stems from a fear of conflict, a desire to please others, or concerns about how others might perceive them. For example, they might take on more tasks than they can manage, become overly involved in their children's lives, or allow others to dictate family decisions. By saying "yes" when they mean "no," they can become overextended, exhausted, and increasingly anxious. This lack of boundary-setting can also affect children, as they may learn to expect unlimited availability and support, leading to dependency rather than independence. In family dynamics, this boundary ambiguity can lead to blurred roles, with anxious parents feeling drained and unfulfilled, struggling to manage their own needs alongside those of their family.

Catastrophising and Negative Thinking

Catastrophising, or the tendency to assume the worst possible outcome in any situation, is a common anxiety-related behavior among anxious parents. Children raised in such environments often adopt this cognitive distortion, leading to increased anxiety and fear (Beck & Clark, 1997). This behavior negatively impacts family dynamics, creating an atmosphere of constant worry where both the parent and child expect negative outcomes, even in benign situations. Over time, this cycle of fear and negativity erodes emotional resilience, leaving both parent and child trapped in a pattern of reassurance-seeking and avoidance, further reinforcing the anxiety.

Sudden Defensive Aggression

Research indicates that individuals with anxiety may exhibit heightened defensive behaviors, including exaggerated aggression, when they feel insecure, or their position is challenged. Studies have shown that anxiety can be associated with increased aggression, particularly in social contexts where individuals perceive threats to their self-esteem or social standing. For instance, anxiety and aggression are linked, noting that individuals with high anxiety levels may display aggressive behaviors as a maladaptive coping mechanism.

Additionally, the use of immature defence mechanisms, such as passive aggression, has been observed in individuals with anxiety. Research published in Frontiers in Psychology highlights that passive aggression is positively connected to other immature defences like splitting and projective identification, which can negatively impact interpersonal relationships.

Furthermore, avoidance behaviors are commonly employed by anxious individuals to evade responsibility or challenging situations. Avoidance coping, which includes behaviors aimed at escaping particular thoughts or feelings, is a significant factor in the maintenance of anxiety. This coping style can prevent individuals from effectively addressing issues, leading to a cycle of anxiety and avoidance. These findings suggest that anxious individuals may respond to insecurity or challenges with defensive behaviors, including exaggerated aggression or avoidance, rather than accepting mistakes or responsibility (Neumann. I. D. et al. 2010, Buglio, G. Lo, at al. 2014)

Avoidance and Lack of Flexibility

Avoidant behavior, often used as a coping mechanism by anxious parents, teaches children to handle fear by avoiding challenging situations. Rapee et al. (2009) found that anxious parents often engage in overprotective parenting, reinforcing avoidance behaviors in their children. As a result, both the mother and child become increasingly reluctant to face new or uncertain experiences, leading to social isolation and stunted emotional development. This lack of flexibility within the family dynamic can severely limit opportunities for personal growth and create a cycle of avoidance that hinders both the parent and child from fully engaging with the world.

Mental Fatigue and Lack of Engagement

Chronic anxiety can lead to mental fatigue, leaving anxious parents emotionally drained and disengaged from their children. Groenewald et al. (2014) suggest that this mental exhaustion can result in emotional withdrawal, leaving the child feeling neglected or unsupported. The parents inability to engage in meaningful or creative activities with their child can weaken the parent-child relationship, leading to feelings of abandonment and emotional disconnection. Over time, this emotional distance can create lasting damage to the family dynamic, as children may struggle to form secure attachments due to a lack of consistent emotional engagement from their anxious parent.

Lack of Resilience and Adaptation

Children of anxious parents often struggle with resilience, as they learn coping mechanisms that prioritise avoidance over emotional regulation. However, resilience is a skill that can be developed through supportive relationships and adaptive coping strategies (Masten & Reed, 2005). Within anxious family environments, intentional efforts to model resilience— such as problem-solving, emotional regulation, and facing fears—can help children build the emotional strength necessary to cope with anxiety. While children of anxious parents may initially struggle to adapt, cultivating resilience through mindful parenting can mitigate the long-term impact of anxiety on their emotional well-being.

Projection and Unresolved Emotional Issues

Anxiety can also drive individuals to offer advice or attempt to manage others' emotional issues as a way of avoiding their own. This behavior, known as projection, often leads anxious individuals to focus on solving other people's problems, sometimes at the expense of addressing their own emotional needs. People with unresolved emotional issues may project their own fears or anxieties onto others, believing that they are offering helpful guidance, when in reality, they are projecting their insecurities. While this may temporarily distract them from their own anxieties, it can also lead to biased or unhelpful advice that does not truly address the needs of the person they are advising.

Conclusion

Anxiety-related behaviors and personality traits in parents can significantly impact family dynamics, shaping the emotional development and resilience of their children. Characteristics such as perfectionism, emotional reactivity, and avoidance not only influence the parents experience of anxiety but also model behaviors that children often internalise. By understanding the influence of anxiety on family relationships, parents can work towards creating a healthier emotional environment, ultimately reducing the transmission of anxiety across generations.

Chapter 10:

The Anxiety Transmission Process

This chapter explores the subtle yet profound mechanisms through which anxiety is transmitted from parents, particularly from mothers, to their children, starting before birth and extending through early childhood. Anxiety is conveyed through intricate biological, emotional, and behavioural pathways, shaping the child's developing emotional framework.

Biological Transmission: Anxiety in the Womb

The transmission of anxiety begins as early as pregnancy, with maternal stress and anxiety influencing fetal development through biological pathways. Stress hormones such as cortisol, released in response to maternal anxiety, cross the placenta and impact the development of the fetal brain. These hormones affect areas like the amygdala, which plays a critical role in emotional regulation and the stress response. High cortisol exposure during pregnancy has been associated with heightened stress sensitivity in children, setting the stage for anxiety disorders later in life.

Research highlights the enduring impact of prenatal anxiety. Studies reveal that children exposed to elevated cortisol levels in utero often exhibit increased fearfulness, hypervigilance, and difficulties in managing stress. The biological groundwork laid during pregnancy creates vulnerabilities that may be further reinforced through postnatal interactions. This underscores the importance of addressing maternal anxiety during pregnancy, as early interventions can mitigate its effects on the child's developing brain.

Neural Mechanisms in Mother-Infant Bonding

The bond between mother and child is critical for a child's emotional security and stress regulation, rooted in intricate neural mechanisms. Key brain regions like the medial preoptic area (MPOA), nucleus accumbens, and amygdala work in concert with neurotransmitters such as oxytocin and dopamine to facilitate maternal behaviors and emotional attachment. Oxytocin, often referred to as the "bonding hormone," enhances maternal sensitivity and promotes trust and connection, while dopamine reinforces caregiving behaviors by associating them with a sense of reward.

When maternal anxiety disrupts these neural processes, it can impair bonding and emotional attunement. An anxious mother may struggle to respond consistently to her child's needs, which can erode the child's sense of security. This can lead to insecure attachment patterns, which are linked to emotional dysregulation and heightened anxiety in children. Supporting mothers in managing their anxiety can strengthen these neural pathways, fostering more secure and nurturing mother-infant bonds.

Behavioural and Social Mechanisms

Emotional Contagion

Children are exceptionally sensitive to their caregivers' emotional states, unconsciously absorbing and mirroring feelings of stress or anxiety. This process, known as emotional contagion, occurs through non-verbal cues such as facial expressions, tone of voice, and body language. For instance, a mother who frequently displays tension or worry may unintentionally transmit these emotions to her child, shaping the child's perception of the world as a threatening place.

Research by Hatfield et al. (1994) highlights how emotional contagion operates within close relationships, showing that children's emotional states often mirror those of their parents. Over time, repeated exposure to a caregiver's anxious emotional signals can condition a child to adopt similar stress responses, increasing their susceptibility to anxiety disorders. Creating emotionally supportive environments is crucial in breaking this cycle, enabling children to develop healthier emotional frameworks.

Modelling and Social Learning

Social learning theory, as proposed by Albert Bandura, emphasises the role of observational learning in shaping behavior. Children often mimic the emotional responses and coping mechanisms modelled by their parents. An anxious parent who avoids social interactions, exhibits hypervigilance, or catastrophises everyday challenges inadvertently teaches their child that such behaviors are appropriate responses to life's uncertainties.

Mineka and Cook's (1988) research on primates demonstrated that fear responses can be learned through observation, illustrating how children internalise anxiety-related behaviors from their parents. This modelling effect perpetuates intergenerational cycles of anxiety and avoidance. Interventions that help parents recognise and modify their own anxious behaviors can significantly reduce the likelihood of these patterns being passed to their children.

Verbal Communication of Fear

Parents' verbal warnings about potential dangers can amplify a child's perception of threat, even in safe environments. For instance, a parent who frequently cautions against talking to strangers or exploring new places may unintentionally instill generalised fears in their child.

Field and Lester (2010) found that children exposed to negative information about novel stimuli were more likely to develop fear responses, highlighting the power of parental language in shaping anxiety. Encouraging balanced communication that emphasises safety without overstating risks can help children build a more realistic and confident approach to the world.

Emotional Transmission: The Unseen Flow

One of the most significant ways maternal anxiety is passed to children is through emotional transmission. Children, especially infants, are acutely attuned to their mothers' emotional states and unconsciously absorb these feelings. When a mother is anxious, her heightened emotional state creates a stressful environment that children instinctively respond to, shaping their own emotional frameworks.

This process often begins with emotional mirroring, where children imitate their mother's emotional responses to stress. For instance, a child who observes their mother reacting with visible tension to minor disruptions, such as a spilled drink or a sudden change in plans, may internalise similar anxious reactions. Over time, these mirrored responses become ingrained, leading to a worldview characterised by heightened sensitivity to stress and fear.

Disruptions in Early Caregiving Routines

Maternal anxiety can disrupt essential caregiving activities, such as establishing sleep routines, consistent soothing, and emotional atonement. An anxious mother may struggle to provide a calm and reassuring presence, which can heighten her child's stress levels and lead to emotional instability.

Tiffany Field's research (2018) demonstrates that maternal anxiety often results in disrupted physical interactions, such as tense body language or inconsistent vocal tones. These disruptions hinder a child's ability to self-soothe and regulate emotions, increasing their vulnerability to anxiety. Addressing maternal anxiety through supportive interventions can help stabilise caregiving routines, promoting emotional security in children.

The Impact of Prenatal Bonding

Maternal anxiety also affects the emotional bond between mother and child during pregnancy. Anxiety can interfere with prenatal bonding, making it difficult for mothers to connect emotionally with their unborn child. This disconnection can lead to insecure attachments after birth, hindering the child's ability to develop a stable emotional foundation.

John Bowlby's attachment theory underscores the importance of secure early relationships in fostering emotional regulation and resilience. Insecure attachments, often resulting from maternal anxiety, are strongly associated with increased risks of anxiety disorders in children. Early interventions aimed at strengthening prenatal and postnatal bonds can help mitigate these risks.

Conclusion

This chapter has explored the intricate mechanisms through which parental anxiety is transmitted to children, encompassing biological, behavioural, and social pathways. Recognising these influences not only provides insights into the development of childhood anxiety but also underscores the importance of early interventions and supportive parenting practices in breaking the cycle.

Part Four:

Pregnancy, Birth & Early Years

Chapter 11:

Anxiety During Pregnancy

<hr/>

The impact of anxiety on a developing child begins long before birth. This chapter explores the profound influence that maternal anxiety during pregnancy has on fetal development, focusing on both biological and emotional pathways. Research demonstrates that a mother's emotional state during pregnancy shapes the child's brain development, emotional regulation, and long-term mental health.

Biological Transmission of Anxiety

During pregnancy, the mother's emotional state has direct, measurable effects on the developing fetus. When a mother experiences high levels of anxiety, her body releases stress hormones, particularly cortisol, as part of the body's natural response to stress. While cortisol is essential for the fetus's development in moderation, prolonged exposure to elevated cortisol levels can have significant consequences for fetal development.

Research on maternal inflammation from *The Inflamed Mind* by Edward Bullmore (2019) highlights how stress-induced inflammation in the mother may affect the fetus's developing stress response systems. This connection between maternal stress and inflammation reveals a biological link to long-term emotional challenges for the child. The inflammatory processes that accompany maternal stress may also contribute to a heightened risk of anxiety in both mothers and their children.

Studies by Vivette Glover and Thomas O'Connor have further demonstrated that maternal stress during pregnancy increases the risk of anxiety disorders in children. Glover's research shows that elevated cortisol levels cross the placenta and directly affect the fetal brain, particularly regions responsible for emotional regulation, such as the amygdala and the hypothalamic-pituitary-adrenal (HPA) axis. Children exposed to high levels of prenatal stress are more likely to experience anxiety and emotional dysregulation later in life.

The Role of Cortisol in Prenatal Development

When a mother experiences chronic anxiety during pregnancy, her body produces elevated levels of cortisol, which can have significant effects on the developing fetus. Cortisol is essential for regulating the body's response to stress, but when present in excessive amounts during pregnancy, it can alter the development of the fetus's hypothalamic-pituitary-adrenal (HPA) axis, the system responsible for managing stress responses.

High levels of prenatal cortisol exposure have been linked to changes in fetal brain development, particularly in regions associated with emotional regulation, such as the amygdala and prefrontal cortex. As a result, children born to mothers who experience high levels of anxiety during pregnancy may be more prone to heightened stress sensitivity and difficulty managing emotions as they grow older. These early biological influences can set the stage for the development of anxiety disorders later in life.

Studies by Vivette Glover have highlighted the impact of prenatal stress on fetal development. Glover's research shows that high maternal cortisol levels during pregnancy can result in long-term changes to a child's stress response system, increasing their risk for anxiety, depression, and emotional regulation difficulties. Additionally, research by Thomas O'Connor supports the finding that maternal anxiety during pregnancy can have lasting effects on a child's ability to manage stress, demonstrating that children exposed to high levels of prenatal stress are more likely to develop emotional difficulties and anxiety-related disorders during childhood and adolescence.

Cortisol is a key hormone involved in the body's stress response. While it is necessary for healthy fetal development, excessive exposure to cortisol can disrupt the development of critical brain regions that manage emotional regulation and stress. Chronic stress in the mother can alter the functioning of the fetus's HPA axis, the system responsible for regulating stress responses.

Disruptions in the HPA axis make the child more sensitive to stress and prone to anxiety disorders later in life. Essentially, when a mother experiences chronic anxiety, her unborn child may be "primed" to be more reactive to stress, laying the groundwork for future emotional and behavioural challenges.

Research by Seymour Levine on maternal separation in rats provides additional insights into how early life stress affects anxiety regulation. Levine's studies show that rat pups experiencing prolonged separation from their mothers exhibit increased stress and anxiety later in life, with disruptions to the HPA axis. This suggests that early bonding disruptions in humans, such as maternal anxiety or postpartum depression, may have similar long-term effects on emotional regulation in children.

Past Trauma and Ongoing Stress

The effects of maternal anxiety are even more pronounced in mothers who have experienced past trauma or ongoing stress. Trauma survivors, especially those with unresolved psychological wounds, are more likely to experience heightened anxiety during pregnancy. This anxiety, fuelled by past experiences of fear or insecurity, increases the risk of pregnancy complications and further disrupts fetal development.

Research into the epigenetic effects of trauma has shown that trauma-related stress in mothers can alter gene expression in the developing fetus, leading to increased susceptibility to stress and emotional dysregulation in later life. Studies on women with histories of trauma, including childhood abuse or exposure to violence, indicate that these mothers are more likely to experience post-traumatic stress disorder (PTSD) during pregnancy, further heightening the stress passed on to their children.

Conclusion

Maternal anxiety during pregnancy has far-reaching implications for both the mother and the developing child. Research shows that when a pregnant mother experiences high levels of anxiety, it can trigger the release of cortisol, a stress hormone that crosses the placenta, influencing the fetus's developing brain. This biological transmission can predispose the child to higher levels of anxiety and emotional dysregulation later in life. Moreover, maternal anxiety can disrupt the emotional bonding process even before birth, potentially affecting the mother-child relationship and the child's ability to form secure attachments in the future.

Addressing maternal anxiety during pregnancy is crucial not only for the mother's well-being but also for the child's long-term emotional resilience. Early intervention, combined with supportive care and strategies such as mindfulness, therapy, and emotional connection, can help mothers manage their anxiety, promote healthier outcomes for themselves and their children, and lay the foundation for secure attachments.

Chapter 12:

Anxiety During the Birth Window

In this chapter, we explore the effects of both C-sections and induced labour on maternal mental health, early childhood health, and the early bonding experience.

The method by which a baby is delivered—whether through Caesarean section (C-section) or induced labour—can significantly influence both the mother's and baby's physical, emotional, and hormonal experiences. These medical interventions, while often lifesaving and necessary, can disrupt the natural processes that typically occur during childbirth. We will examine how the altered hormonal pathways in these methods can affect the mother's emotional state and the baby's development.

The choice of Cesarean delivery childbirth

Pregnancy-specific anxiety can be a significant factor influencing elective caesarean sections, according to recent research (Slade et al, 2020) However, the evidence for its impact on induced labour interventions is less clear. A study of 1,874 pregnant women found that anxiety in the second trimester was a significant predictor for elective cesarean section.

The overall elective cesarean section rate in this study was 45%. Factors contributing to this association may include Women with pregnancy-specific anxiety, especially fear of childbirth, doubting their ability to deliver naturally, Anxious women feeling less capable and having less confidence in obstetric staff, and Anxiety exacerbating fear of childbirth, leading to preference for caesarean section. Interestingly, maternal age and education level indirectly affected the choice of elective caesarean section by influencing pregnancy-specific anxiety. Younger women and those with lower educational levels were more vulnerable to pregnancy-specific anxiety.

Studies, including Sun (2019) and a large one by Michigan Medicine (contemporary Clinic), found that women with prenatal anxiety or depression had a higher likelihood of having a cesarean delivery, even when they were otherwise at low risk for the procedure. The anxiety often centres around concerns about the childbirth process, leading some mothers and healthcare providers to opt for a cesarean section as a perceived safer or less stressful option.

In another study, pregnancy-specific anxiety was identified as a significant factor influencing elective caesarean sections, especially when the anxiety was related to concerns about childbirth or the health of the baby. Women with higher levels of anxiety were more likely to choose or be advised to undergo caesarean delivery (PLOS). This connection between maternal anxiety and caesarean sections highlights the importance of addressing perinatal mood disorders to ensure that caesarean decisions are based on clinical needs rather than psychological factors.

Cultural influence

Cultural beliefs, especially in certain communities, can significantly influence the decision to deliver a baby by cesarean section, often aligning the birth with auspicious dates or avoiding "bad" astrological days. In countries like India, China, and parts of Southeast Asia, astrology plays a central role in life events, including childbirth. Parents may opt for an elective cesarean section to ensure their child is born on a day or at a time considered astrologically favourable, believing it will bring health, success, and prosperity to the child.

For example, in India, certain dates or times, known as muhurtas, are believed to be more auspicious according to Vedic astrology. Similarly, many parents aim to avoid periods associated with bad omens, such as Rahu Kaal or Shani influence, which are considered inauspicious for new beginnings. In China, many people select auspicious dates based on the Lunar calendar, particularly during the festival season or when Feng Shui principles indicate good fortune.

In such contexts, elective cesarean sections are chosen to ensure the baby is born at a specific "lucky" time, regardless of medical necessity. This cultural practice has gained prevalence in urban areas where access to cesarean deliveries is easier. However, it has raised concerns in the medical community due to the increased risks associated with unnecessary cesarean sections (Michigan Medicine - Contemporary Clinic).

This cultural influence demonstrates how deeply embedded traditional beliefs can shape medical decisions, sometimes overriding clinical advice in favour of spiritual or astrological considerations.

Child impact of Cesarean delivery

The case for cesarean delivery is often based on medical necessity and safety. It can be life-saving for both mother and child in situations such as fetal distress, placental complications, or when labour does not progress naturally. Cesarean sections may also be scheduled for maternal health concerns, previous cesarean deliveries, or to prevent complications in complex vaginal births. However, significant concerns exist about the overuse of cesareans. Unnecessary cesareans can increase risks of infections, blood clots, and result in longer recovery periods for the mother. Babies born via cesarean may face respiratory issues and miss out on the beneficial exposure to microbiota during vaginal birth. The rising trend of elective cesareans, driven by convenience or cultural factors, has raised concerns about long-term effects on maternal and child health. While cesareans are essential in emergencies, their overuse without medical justification has become a growing public health issue.

The following section will discuss the potential drawbacks of cesarean births, focusing on the hormonal shifts and emotional bonding influenced by a lack of natural birth hormones, the missing birth canal compression, the microbiome factor, and the emotional impact of reduced skin-to-skin contact after delivery.

Hormonal Shifts and Emotional Bonding

One of the most significant differences between a natural vaginal delivery and a C-section is the hormonal cascade that occurs during childbirth. During a vaginal birth, the mother's body naturally releases high levels of oxytocin, often called the "love hormone." Oxytocin is critical for several reasons: it facilitates uterine contractions, helps expel the placenta, and plays a crucial role in postpartum recovery. More importantly, oxytocin promotes emotional bonding between mother and child, enhancing feelings of closeness and affection that are vital for the establishment of a secure emotional attachment.

In contrast, C-sections—especially those that are unplanned or performed in emergency situations—may disrupt the natural hormonal flow that accompanies vaginal birth. This disruption can result in lower oxytocin levels in the mother immediately after birth. Without the surge of oxytocin that typically occurs during vaginal delivery, some mothers may find it harder to feel the immediate emotional connection with their newborn. This delay in bonding can contribute to feelings of emotional disconnection, which may heighten the risk of postpartum anxiety or depression.

Hormonal Disruption

Michel Odent, a pioneer in the field of childbirth and maternal health, has extensively studied how different birth methods, particularly C-sections, affect the hormonal and emotional experiences of mothers. Odent's research emphasises the importance of the hormonal cascade that takes place during natural childbirth, particularly the role of oxytocin in creating the emotional conditions for bonding between mother and child. He suggests that when this natural process is interrupted—such as in a C-section—the mother's hormonal balance is altered, potentially leading to delays in bonding and increased vulnerability to postpartum depression and anxiety.

Odent also argues that C-sections, especially when performed under stressful or emergency conditions, may exacerbate maternal stress, compounding the emotional and psychological strain on the mother. The absence of labour, which naturally prepares the mother for the transition to postpartum life, can leave some mothers feeling emotionally unprepared for the sudden arrival of their baby. This can lead to feelings of inadequacy, heightened worry, or a sense of emotional detachment, which are all contributing factors to postpartum anxiety.

Baby's Emotional and Physical Health

The effects of a C-section are not limited to the mother; they also extend to the baby's emotional and physical health. While C-sections are often necessary to ensure the safety of the mother and child, they can disrupt several key processes that occur during a natural vaginal delivery, particularly those related to the baby's physical health and stress regulation.

The Missing Birth Canal Compression

During a vaginal delivery, the baby passes through the birth canal, where the natural compression helps to clear the baby's lungs of fluid and prepares the baby to breathe air. This process also provides a form of physical stress that helps the baby transition from the womb to the outside world. In C-section deliveries, however, the baby does not experience this compression, which can result in respiratory issues or delayed lung function. Babies born via C-section may require extra monitoring or interventions to ensure that their breathing is stable, adding stress to the mother-baby dyad in the immediate postpartum period.

The Microbiome Factor

Another critical aspect of vaginal birth is the baby's exposure to the mother's vaginal microbiome—the beneficial bacteria that colonise the baby's skin, mouth, and gut as they pass through the birth canal. This exposure plays a key role in the development of the baby's immune system and contributes to long-term health outcomes. Babies born via C-section miss out on this natural transfer of beneficial bacteria, which can leave them at higher risk for immune-related issues, such as allergies or asthma, as well as digestive disorders.

Recent research also suggests that the gut microbiome is closely linked to emotional and cognitive development, with emerging evidence indicating that a healthy microbiome can play a role in reducing stress and anxiety. Babies who miss this initial microbiome transfer may have a different developmental trajectory when it comes to their emotional health, potentially contributing to a heightened stress response or an increased risk of anxiety as they grow.

Emotional Impact of the Birth Experience

The process of birth is a significant emotional event for both mother and baby. The stress of a C-section, particularly one that occurs under emergency circumstances, can create a heightened sense of anxiety for the mother, which the baby may also experience. Babies are highly attuned to their mother's emotional state, and when a mother is experiencing stress or anxiety, the baby can absorb these emotions, both during the birth process and in the immediate postpartum period. This can contribute to a heightened stress response in the baby, potentially leading to increased irritability, difficulty soothing, or trouble with feeding and sleeping.

Practical Insight: Given the potential emotional and physical challenges associated with C-sections, it is important to focus on strategies that can help mitigate the impact on both mother and baby. One of the most effective ways to promote emotional bonding and reduce anxiety after a C-section is through skin-to-skin contact immediately after birth.

Skin-to-Skin Contact

Skin-to-skin contact involves placing the baby directly on the mother's chest immediately after birth, allowing the mother and baby to experience each other's warmth, touch, and smell. This practice has been shown to promote the release of oxytocin, even in mothers who have had C-sections, helping to compensate for the hormonal disruption that may have occurred during the surgical procedure. Skin-to-skin contact also helps regulate the baby's body temperature, heart rate, and breathing, and it encourages early breastfeeding initiation, which further supports bonding.

In many hospitals and birthing centres, family-cantered C-sections are becoming more common. These practices aim to create a more natural and supportive environment for both mother and baby, even during a surgical birth. Family-cantered C-sections may include modifications such as:

- Allowing the mother to hold her baby immediately after birth, even in the operating room, to promote early skin-to-skin contact.
- Encouraging early breastfeeding initiation while the mother is still in recovery, which can help establish the breastfeeding relationship and promote bonding.
- Creating a calm and supportive atmosphere in the operating room, with dimmed lights, soothing music, or a quieter environment to reduce stress for both mother and baby.

These practices can help bridge the gap between the physiological and emotional experiences of a natural birth and a C-section, promoting emotional bonding and reducing the likelihood of postpartum anxiety.

Induced labour

Regarding induced labour interventions, the available research does not provide clear evidence of a direct link with pregnancy-specific anxiety. One study found that anxiety and pregnancy-specific stress were not directly associated with the duration of stage 1 labour (Slade, 2020). However, there was an indirect effect: elevated pregnancy-specific stress led to greater use of epidurals, which was linked to increased rates of augmentation and longer labour duration.

For anxious mothers, the decision to opt for induced labour often stems from a desire for control and predictability. The unpredictable nature of spontaneous labour, combined with the fears associated with maternal anxiety, can create significant emotional stress. Induced labour offers a degree of certainty—mothers know when the process will begin, which can alleviate some of the anxiety around the timing and unpredictability of childbirth. For mothers with heightened anxiety, particularly those who have experienced traumatic births or complications in the past, this sense of control can offer psychological relief, reducing the emotional burden of waiting for natural labour to begin.

In addition to the desire for control, anxious mothers may also fear potential complications if the pregnancy continues beyond their due date. Concerns about stillbirth, fetal distress, or the risks of post-term pregnancy can push some mothers toward requesting induction to reduce perceived risks. Although these fears may not always align with medical necessity, maternal anxiety can amplify such concerns, influencing decision-making. Conversations with healthcare providers are crucial in these situations to ensure that the decision for induction is based on a balance of emotional well-being and medical necessity rather than solely anxiety-driven fears.

However, it's important to recognise that induced labour is not without its risks, which may further contribute to maternal anxiety. Induction can lead to more intense contractions, a longer labour process, and an increased likelihood of medical interventions such as cesarean sections. Anxious mothers should be encouraged to explore their concerns with healthcare professionals to fully understand the risks and benefits of induction. Addressing these anxieties early in the pregnancy, through therapy or support systems, can help anxious mothers feel more empowered in their decision-making process, ensuring a smoother and less stressful labour experience.

Conclusion

The method by which a baby enters the world significantly influences both the immediate and long-term physical, emotional, and hormonal experiences for the mother and the baby. While Caesarean sections (C-sections) are often medically necessary and can be life-saving, they disrupt the natural hormonal cascade associated with childbirth. This disruption can hinder the natural release of oxytocin, often referred to as the "love hormone," which plays a crucial role in bonding between mother and child. The absence or reduction of oxytocin release in C-sections may contribute to maternal anxiety and delays in emotional bonding, affecting the overall emotional connection during the critical postpartum period.

Similarly, induced labour, while necessary in some cases, can alter the typical childbirth process by accelerating labour artificially. This can intensify contractions, creating heightened stress for both mother and baby. The accelerated process of induced labour may interfere with the gradual hormonal shifts that typically aid in postpartum recovery and bonding. Both methods of delivery—C-sections and induced labour—can affect not only the mother's mental health but also the baby's emotional and physical health. Understanding these dynamics is vital in providing mothers with the necessary support to minimise the potential risks of postpartum anxiety, emotional disconnection, and other mental health challenges.

Chapter 13:

Postpartum Anxiety

───── ◠ ⁂ ◠ ─────

This chapter explores the profound impact of postpartum (postnatal) anxiety on emotional bonding, the mother-child relationship, and the long-term development of the child.

Postpartum Anxiety

The postpartum period is often idealised as a time of joy and bonding for new mothers, yet for many women, it is a period of heightened vulnerability and emotional turmoil. While adjusting to the physical and psychological demands of motherhood, many mothers experience significant stress, anxiety, and even depression. Postpartum anxiety, although less discussed than postpartum depression (PPD), is a common and serious condition that affects both mother and child. By examining the nature of postpartum anxiety, its relationship with PPD, and its effects on maternal behavior, this chapter highlights the importance of early intervention to support both the mother and the baby.

Probability of vulnerability

Mothers who are already severely anxious are at a higher risk of developing postpartum depression (PPD) and postpartum anxiety (PPA). Research evidence underscores the significant role of prenatal anxiety in increasing the risk of postpartum depression (PPD) and postpartum anxiety (PPA). Longitudinal studies, such as those by Faisal-Cury et al. (2008), demonstrate that untreated anxiety during pregnancy can transition into postpartum psychological challenges, with women exhibiting higher levels of depressive symptoms. Similarly, Biaggi et al. (2016) highlighted the need for early detection and management of severe prenatal anxiety, as it is a critical factor in the onset of both PPD and PPA. The biological pathways underlying this association are also pivotal; Yim et al. (2015) and Field (2017) emphasise the dysregulation of the hypothalamic-pituitary-adrenal (HPA) axis caused by elevated stress hormones like cortisol, further exacerbating vulnerability to postpartum mood disorders.

Behavioural and environmental factors compound the risk, with anxious mothers often perceiving postpartum stressors as insurmountable. Dennis et al. (2009) identified maternal anxiety as a key factor in amplifying the challenges of infant care and sleep deprivation, contributing to heightened rates of PPD and PPA. Studies like Matthey et al. (2003) reveal that a history of anxiety disorders nearly doubles the likelihood of postpartum anxiety, underscoring how pre-existing conditions heighten sensitivity to early motherhood stressors. Additionally, comorbid anxiety and depression, as reported by Stuart-Parrigon and Stuart (2014), exacerbate the severity of postpartum mood disorders. Beck's (2001) meta-analysis reinforces the predictive value of antenatal anxiety, establishing it as a critical focus area for preventative care and intervention during pregnancy.

Postpartum Depression and Anxiety

Postpartum anxiety and postpartum depression are often interconnected, co-existing and exacerbating one another. While postpartum depression has gained significant visibility, postpartum anxiety remains less discussed despite being equally pervasive. Mothers experiencing postpartum anxiety often face excessive worry, persistent fear, and feelings of inadequacy, which are common symptoms of depression as well. Research shows that many women suffering from PPD also display signs of anxiety, leading to a compounded emotional struggle.

Postpartum anxiety manifests in various ways. For some mothers, it involves an overwhelming sense of responsibility for the baby's safety, health, and well-being, while others experience intrusive thoughts about potential dangers. These irrational fears can cause significant emotional distress and contribute to feelings of shame and guilt. Mothers may feel they are failing their child or that they are unfit to be caregivers, further fuelling their anxiety.

Understanding Postpartum Anxiety

Postpartum anxiety is more than just typical parental worry; it is an excessive, irrational fear that can interfere with a mother's ability to care for her child. Mothers with postpartum anxiety often find themselves trapped in a state of hypervigilance, constantly checking on their baby or worrying about minor issues like feeding or sleep schedules. This heightened state of alertness can lead to emotional exhaustion and a sense of inadequacy in their role as a mother.

Some women experience intrusive thoughts—unwanted, distressing thoughts about possible harm coming to the baby. Although these thoughts are typically irrational, they cause immense emotional distress and lead to further feelings of guilt or unworthiness. Mothers may feel overwhelmed by these anxieties, fearing they are incapable of protecting or adequately caring for their child.

The Overlap with Postpartum Depression

While postpartum anxiety and postpartum depression are distinct conditions, they frequently overlap. Research suggests that mothers who experience high levels of anxiety during the postpartum period are at greater risk of developing depression. The combination of anxiety and depression exacerbates emotional distress, making it harder for mothers to seek help or engage in self-care. They may feel trapped, unable to manage their emotions or care for their baby properly.

Mothers suffering from both postpartum anxiety and depression may struggle with sleep, even when their baby is resting. They often feel disconnected from their baby and experience irritability, hopelessness, and emotional withdrawal. These challenges hinder the bonding process, making it difficult for mothers to establish a secure emotional attachment with their child.

Extreme Variations

In more severe cases, postpartum anxiety and depression can cause mothers to feel detached from their baby or even reject them. Some mothers may refuse to feed or cuddle their baby, worry excessively about their body post-birth, or feel consumed by guilt over their perceived failures as a mother. These behaviours are often linked to the hormonal changes and emotional strain experienced during the postpartum period.

Research indicates that about 17% of women experience postpartum anxiety in the first few months after giving birth, while 10-15% develop postpartum depression (BMC, PostpartumDepression.org). Factors such as a history of mental health issues, lack of social support, and difficult childbirth experiences increase the risk of postpartum anxiety and depression.

Research on Maternal Anxiety

Cheryl Tatano Beck's (2001) extensive research on maternal anxiety and postpartum mood disorders has played a critical role in understanding the impact of these conditions on mothers and their interactions with their babies. Beck's Postpartum Depression Screening Scale (PDSS) has been instrumental in diagnosing postpartum depression and anxiety. Her qualitative studies explore how traumatic childbirth experiences, anxiety, and depression contribute to maternal disconnection, difficulty with breastfeeding, and bonding struggles.

Beck emphasises that untreated anxiety and depression can lead some mothers to avoid or reject contact with their baby due to feelings of inadequacy, guilt, or fear of not meeting societal expectations of motherhood. In more severe cases, mothers may experience postpartum PTSD, which can occur even in medically uncomplicated births when the mother perceives her experience as traumatic. Left unaddressed, these emotional struggles disrupt maternal bonding and can have long-term psychological effects on both mother and child.

Diana Lynn Barnes and Cheryl Beck have extensively explored the connection between postpartum anxiety and depression. Barnes' work highlights how untreated anxiety can heighten the risk of developing depression, worsening the mother's emotional state. Beck's research shows that unresolved postpartum anxiety and depression can have long-term consequences for both mother and child. Children of mothers who experience these conditions are more likely to develop behavioural problems, attachment disorders, and emotional dysregulation as they grow.

Beck's findings also underscore the intergenerational transmission of anxiety and emotional challenges. When maternal anxiety and depression go untreated, the child often mirrors the mother's emotional state, leading to a cycle of anxiety that may persist into adolescence and adulthood. Early recognition and treatment of postpartum anxiety are essential to prevent long-term emotional and developmental issues for children.

One of the most significant effects of postpartum anxiety is its disruption of the bonding process between mother and baby. Bonding is essential for early emotional development, laying the foundation for a secure attachment.

The Role of Anxiety in Disrupting Bonding

Mothers with postpartum anxiety may feel emotionally disconnected from their baby, struggling to find joy or fulfillment in caregiving. This disconnection manifests in several ways:

- *Avoidance of physical contact*: Some anxious mothers may avoid holding or breastfeeding their baby due to fears of doing it incorrectly or concerns that something could go wrong.

- *Difficulty soothing the baby*: An anxious mother may struggle to calm her baby, as her emotional state prevents her from responding confidently. Babies are highly attuned to their mother's emotions, and when the mother is anxious, the baby may become anxious as well. This creates a cycle of emotional dysregulation for both.

- *Hypervigilance and overprotectiveness:* In contrast to emotional withdrawal, some mothers may become overly protective, constantly checking on their baby or overreacting to minor concerns. While rooted in care, this hypervigilance can create a stressful environment that hinders natural bonding.

Recognising the Signs of Postpartum Anxiety

Early recognition of postpartum anxiety is critical to preventing long-term emotional and developmental issues. Healthcare providers, family members, and mothers themselves should be aware of key symptoms of postpartum anxiety, such as:

- Persistent worry about the baby's safety.
- Difficulty sleeping, even when the baby is asleep.
- Feeling overwhelmed by caregiving responsibilities.
- Avoidance of contact with the baby or emotional disconnection.
- Irrational fears or intrusive thoughts.

Encouraging mothers to seek help at the first signs of anxiety can prevent escalation and support a healthier postpartum experience for both mother and baby.

Conclusion

Postpartum anxiety is a common but often under-recognised condition that can significantly impact both mother and baby. If left untreated, it can interfere with bonding, hinder the mother's ability to care for her child, and lead to long-term emotional and developmental challenges. However, by recognising the signs of postpartum anxiety early and seeking help, mothers can manage their symptoms and foster a healthy emotional connection with their baby.

Chapter 14:

The Mother as The Primary

Caregiver

This chapter revisits and highlights the crucial contributions of mothers as primary caregivers, examining the various forces that reinforce and sustain this role.

The role of the mother as the primary caregiver is shaped by a dynamic combination of biological, social, cultural, and legal factors. These influences work together to create the framework within which mothers assume the primary caregiving role, a position central to the development and well-being of children. Through an exploration of the biological bonds formed through childbirth, societal expectations, cultural norms, and legal structures, the chapter underscores the enduring significance of maternal caregiving in the broader context of family and child development.

How the Mother Becomes the Primary Caregiver

Throughout history and in modern societies, mothers are often expected to assume caregiving responsibilities due to these intertwined influences. Mothers often become the primary caregivers naturally due to their direct involvement in pregnancy, childbirth, and breastfeeding. Biologically, women are inherently predisposed to caregiving roles through hormonal and physiological mechanisms that support maternal bonding and caregiving behaviours.

As already captured in previous chapters the process begins in pregnancy, when oxytocin, a hormone linked to bonding and maternal behaviours, begins to circulate in higher levels. Oxytocin levels spike during childbirth, promoting bonding between mother and child. This hormonal response makes the mother particularly attuned to her child's needs, encouraging nurturing and caregiving from the moment of birth. Breastfeeding further strengthens this bond, as oxytocin is released in the mother during nursing, enhancing the emotional connection between mother and child. This biological inclination lays the foundation for the mother to become the child's primary source of care, comfort, and emotional security.

Biological Expectations

From a biological perspective, the mother's role as a primary caregiver is supported by evolutionary and hormonal factors.

Hormonal Influence: The role of oxytocin cannot be overstated when examining maternal behavior. Known as the "love hormone," oxytocin is responsible for stimulating labour, milk production, and fostering emotional bonds. Studies show that when mothers engage in skin-to-skin contact and breastfeeding, this hormone further strengthens the mother-child bond, reinforcing the caregiving relationship.

Evolutionary Perspectives: From an evolutionary standpoint, mothers have traditionally been the primary source of food, comfort, and protection for infants. Evolutionary psychology suggests that children are biologically wired to stay close to their mothers for survival, while mothers have an innate drive to protect and nurture their young. This biological blueprint for survival has cemented the mother's role as the central figure in a child's early life. Anthropologically, mothers ensured the child's survival through breastfeeding and constant care, while also providing emotional security during the vulnerable early years of life.

Neurobiological Responses: The maternal brain undergoes specific changes during pregnancy and postpartum that enable mothers to be more sensitive to their child's needs. The amygdala, responsible for processing emotions, becomes more active, making mothers more attuned to their baby's cues like crying or smiling. This responsiveness is critical in ensuring that the child receives consistent care and emotional support, which is vital for healthy development.

Social and Cultural Conventions and Expectations

Socially and culturally, the mother's role as the primary caregiver has been shaped by traditional gender roles and societal expectations. Across many cultures, caregiving is largely seen as a woman's responsibility, especially in the early years of a child's life.

Traditional Gender Roles: Historically, caregiving has been viewed as a natural extension of a woman's role in the family. In many societies, men were seen as the breadwinners while women were tasked with domestic duties, including raising children. This view is reinforced by longstanding beliefs that women are inherently more nurturing and emotionally attuned to their children's needs. As a result, the mother has traditionally been positioned as the central figure in a child's upbringing, particularly in societies where patriarchal values dominate.

Cultural Expectations: In many cultures, there is an idealisation of motherhood that promotes the view that a mother should prioritise her children's well-being above all else. For example, in Asian, Middle Eastern, and Latin American cultures, the mother is often seen as the heart of the family, responsible not only for the physical well-being of the child but also for their emotional and moral development. In these cultures, the extended family may assist, but the mother's central role remains culturally and socially reinforced.

In Western cultures, although gender roles are evolving and fathers are increasingly more involved in child-rearing, the mother is still often viewed as the primary emotional caregiver. Media portrayals and societal narratives around "good motherhood" further reinforce these expectations, where mothers are expected to be attentive, nurturing, and emotionally available to their children at all times.

Workplace and Policy Influences: In many societies, maternity leave policies far exceed paternity leave, which can reinforce the expectation that the mother will be the primary caregiver, especially during the early years of the child's life. In countries like Australia, where maternity leave policies provide more time off for mothers than fathers, it becomes socially normalised for mothers to take on the primary caregiving role. Additionally, societal infrastructure such as limited access to affordable childcare can further perpetuate this dynamic, as many women may feel they have no choice but to remain the primary caregiver while fathers return to work.

Legal Implications Mother as the Primary Caregiver

In legal contexts, particularly in matters of family law, the role of the mother as the primary caregiver has significant implications, especially in cases of custody disputes or shared parenting arrangements.

In both the United States and the United Kingdom, the role of the mother as the primary caregiver has legal implications, particularly in the context of custody disputes and family law. In the U.S., the courts generally do not automatically assume that the mother will be the primary caregiver but instead base custody decisions on the "best interests of the child" standard. This includes evaluating factors like the parent-child relationship, the emotional and physical well-being of the child, and the ability of each parent to provide a stable environment.

Historically, mothers have been favoured as primary caregivers, especially for younger children, due to their traditional caregiving roles, but modern family law aims to balance caregiving between both parents, acknowledging that fathers can play an equally important role. However, conflicts often arise when one parent feels they are not given equal responsibility or time with the child, leading to legal battles over custody arrangements.

In the UK, similar legal principles apply, with courts focusing on the welfare of the child as the paramount concern. Under the Children Act 1989, both parents have parental responsibility, and there is no legal presumption in favour of mothers as primary caregivers. Instead, the court evaluates which arrangement best serves the child's welfare, considering factors like continuity of care, the child's attachment to each parent, and the parents' ability to meet the child's emotional and developmental needs. Although shared parenting is encouraged, conflicts can occur when mothers, who often assume primary caregiving roles, fear losing control or time with their child in the event of a custody dispute. This can create tension between the evolving legal framework that promotes shared responsibility and traditional expectations of motherhood as the primary caregiving role.

Australian law

Family Law in Australia: The Family Law Act 1975 in Australia is the primary legal framework governing parenting disputes. The Act emphasises the "best interests of the child" as the paramount consideration in custody and parenting arrangements. While the law does not automatically favour mothers as primary caregivers, in practice, the court often considers caregiving history and emotional bonds when making custody decisions. If the mother has historically been the primary caregiver, courts are likely to maintain this status quo to avoid disrupting the child's emotional security.

Shared Parental Responsibility: Australian family law promotes shared parental responsibility, encouraging both parents to remain actively involved in their child's life. This principle is designed to ensure that the child maintains relationships with both parents, provided that it is in their best interests. However, where the mother has been the primary caregiver, especially in the early years, courts often recognise the need to maintain this dynamic, as long as it provides stability and security for the child.

Legal Conflicts: Legal conflicts can arise when one parent, typically the father, seeks greater involvement or when the mother's ability to care for the child is questioned due to circumstances like mental health challenges, such as maternal anxiety. Courts must balance the child's right to a secure emotional environment with the practicalities of shared parenting, often leading to complex decisions around custody and caregiving roles.

In some cases, the mother's role as the primary caregiver may come into conflict with the legal principle of equal parenting time. While shared parenting is encouraged, it may not always be feasible, especially in cases where the mother is still breastfeeding or where the child has a particularly strong emotional bond with the mother. Legal decisions in these cases often aim to balance the mother's established caregiving role with the child's need for stability and ongoing relationships with both parents.

Mental Health and Custody: In cases where a mother is struggling with severe anxiety or other mental health issues, her role as the primary caregiver may be reassessed. Courts may consider whether the mother's mental health is affecting her ability to provide a stable and nurturing environment. In such situations, courts may grant greater caregiving responsibilities to the father or other caregivers to ensure the child's emotional and physical needs are met.

Conclusion

The role of the mother as the primary caregiver is shaped by a combination of biological, social, cultural, and legal factors. While biological and evolutionary mechanisms support the mother's caregiving role, cultural norms and societal expectations reinforce this dynamic. However, the evolving legal framework, particularly in Australia, seeks to balance traditional caregiving roles with modern principles of shared parental responsibility, aiming to ensure the best interests of the child are met.

Part Five:

Early Roots of Childhood Anxiety

Chapter 15:

Planting Early Emotional Seeds of Anxiety

─────── ❦ ───────

Infants and young children are incredibly sensitive to their environment, particularly to the emotional signals they receive from their primary caregivers. Long before they can fully understand or articulate their emotions, children absorb anxiety and stress through the subtle, non-verbal interactions they experience daily with their mothers. This chapter explores how parental anxiety can be transmitted to children through these early interactions, embedding emotional patterns that may persist into adolescence and adulthood.

Non-Verbal Emotional Transmission

One of the most profound ways that anxiety is passed from mother to child in early life is through non-verbal emotional transmission. From the very first months of life, infants are highly attuned to their caregivers' emotional states, even when those emotions are not explicitly expressed. A mother's body language, facial expressions, tone of voice, and overall demeanour send powerful signals that shape how a baby perceives the world around them. For an anxious mother, these signals often reflect her internal state of tension, worry, or fear. Infants, in turn, pick up on these cues and may begin to mirror their mother's anxiety in their own behavior and emotional responses.

Non-Verbal Cues in Emotional Development

Non-verbal communication is the primary way in which infants interpret their environment and make sense of the emotions of those around them. For example, an anxious mother may unknowingly transmit her anxiety through:

- Tense body language, such as stiff shoulders or jittery movements, which can signal to the baby that something is wrong or that the environment is unsafe.
- Reduced eye contact, which may make the baby feel emotionally disconnected or uncertain about their mother's presence and support.
- Quick, shallow breathing patterns, which can increase stress levels in the baby, as infants are highly sensitive to the rhythm and tone of their mother's breathing.

Over time, these non-verbal cues can shape how the baby perceives the world and responds to stress. Babies learn to interpret these emotional signals as indicators of whether their environment is safe or dangerous, and when a mother's non-verbal cues consistently convey anxiety, the baby may internalise this stress and develop an anxious outlook on the world.

Tiffany Field's research (2018) on maternal behavior and infant emotional development highlights the powerful role that non-verbal communication plays in shaping a baby's emotional responses. Field's studies demonstrate that infants of anxious mothers are more likely to exhibit stress-related behaviors—such as irritability, difficulty soothing, or excessive crying—when exposed to their mother's tense body language, reduced eye contact, and other anxiety-driven cues. These findings suggest that babies mirror the anxiety they observe in their mothers, creating a feedback loop of emotional stress that can affect their long-term emotional development.

Physical Cues and Emotional Regulation

In the earliest stages of life, infants rely heavily on physical interactions with their caregivers to regulate their emotions. Holding, feeding, and soothing are not just physical acts— they are critical to the development of a baby's emotional and psychological stability. For mothers who struggle with anxiety, however, these interactions may become inconsistent or strained, leading to dysregulation in the baby's emotional responses.

The Impact of Anxious Physical Interactions

Anxious mothers may find it difficult to maintain the nurturing, soothing behaviours that are essential for a baby's emotional security. Physical cues, such as eye contact, gentle touch, and calm, rhythmic movements, play a vital role in helping infants regulate their stress and emotions. When a mother is overwhelmed by anxiety, she may struggle to provide consistent nurturing behaviours, which can result in increased stress for the infant.

For example, a mother who feels anxious may avoid prolonged eye contact during feedings or holding sessions, which can make the baby feel insecure or emotionally disconnected. A mother who fidgets nervously or shifts her baby frequently while holding them may unintentionally create a sense of instability, signalling to the baby that the environment is unpredictable or unsafe.

An anxious mother's inconsistent responses to her baby's cries or distress—either through emotional withdrawal or overreaction—can make it difficult for the baby to develop a sense of emotional security, leading to increased stress and difficulty with self-soothing.

These physical interactions are critical because they provide the baby with a sense of emotional safety and predictability. When a mother's anxiety interferes with these physical cues, the baby may have difficulty learning how to regulate their own emotions, which can have long-term effects on their emotional development.

Meaney's studies (2001) on maternal care in rats provide crucial insights into how early interactions between mother and offspring affect anxiety regulation. His work focuses on how high-licking and grooming behaviors in rat mothers contribute to lower stress levels in their offspring, while low maternal care results in elevated anxiety. The following are the findings:

- **Epigenetic changes:** Meaney's research demonstrates that maternal behavior affects the expression of genes involved in regulating the stress response, specifically the glucocorticoid receptor gene in the hippocampus. This change results in long-lasting effects on how offspring manage stress and anxiety.

- **Long-term impacts**: Pups receiving high maternal care show better stress regulation and lower anxiety levels later in life, highlighting how early nurturing behaviors have profound implications for emotional development.

Daily Interactions and Emotional Learning

Babies and young children learn how to regulate their emotions by watching how their mothers respond to everyday stressors. From a very young age, children are like emotional sponges, absorbing the behaviors and emotional patterns they observe in their caregivers. When a mother consistently displays anxiety-driven behaviors—such as overreacting to minor stressors, displaying frustration or worry, or withdrawing emotionally—her child may begin to internalise these behaviors and adopt similar patterns.

Emotional learning begins long before children can articulate their feelings. Infants and toddlers watch their mothers closely to understand how to react to the world around them, and these observations lay the groundwork for how they manage stress and regulate their emotions later in life. For example:

If a mother frequently overreacts to minor stresses—such as rushing to soothe the baby at the slightest sound or expressing visible frustration when things go wrong—the child may learn to view the world as unpredictable or overwhelming, leading to a heightened stress response.

On the other hand, if a mother withdraws emotionally during times of stress—perhaps avoiding physical contact, becoming silent, or distancing herself from the child—the baby may feel emotionally unsupported, which can contribute to insecure attachment and difficulties with emotional regulation.

Over time, these daily interactions teach children how to cope with stress. If a child learns that the appropriate response to stress is either excessive worry or emotional withdrawal, they may struggle to develop healthy coping mechanisms, leading to anxiety-related behaviors as they grow older.

Conclusion

The emotional patterns that children absorb from their mothers during these early interactions can have long-lasting effects on their emotional health. Children who are exposed to a high level of maternal anxiety may grow up with a heightened sense of vigilance, constantly scanning their environment for potential threats or feeling unsure of how to manage their emotions in stressful situations. These early emotional seeds of anxiety, if not addressed, can contribute to the development of anxiety disorders, behavioural challenges, and emotional dysregulation in later childhood and adolescence.

Chapter 16

Critical Stages of Vulnerability for Children

―――― ⌒❄⌒ ――――

Research in psychology and neuroscience has consistently demonstrated that the early years of a child's life are critical for personality development, with many experts estimating that around 80% of a child's personality is shaped by the age of seven. This period is characterised by rapid emotional, psychological, and neurobiological growth, during which children absorb and internalise vast amounts of information from their environment. In this chapter, we will explore how parental anxiety can influence children during these sensitive stages, making them more vulnerable to long-term emotional and behavioural issues.

Early Childhood and Personality Development

According to Dr. Bruce Lipton, a leading cell biologist and author of The Biology of Belief (2005), children operate predominantly in a state of brain activity known as Theta brainwaves during their first seven years. This state, akin to hypnosis, allows children to absorb behavioural patterns, emotional responses, and beliefs from their environment without conscious filtering. Children act like sponges, copying the actions and emotions of their caregivers, family members, and peers. Lipton's research suggests that these early experiences effectively "program" the unconscious mind, shaping how individuals respond to stress, relationships, and daily life challenges well into adulthood.

During this developmental phase, the unconscious mind is highly receptive, storing a vast array of behavioural "programs" that stem from repeated exposure to the dynamics of the home, social interactions, and cultural norms. This means that the emotional states and coping mechanisms modelled by a child's mother are likely to become ingrained behaviours in the child, with significant implications for their future emotional regulation and mental health.

The Unconscious Mind & Behavioural Programs

Children up to age seven lack the fully developed critical thinking abilities found in the prefrontal cortex, which governs executive functioning. As a result, they rely heavily on the unconscious mind to process and make sense of the world. During this period, the unconscious mind absorbs the emotional climate of the home, particularly the behavior and reactions of the mother, who typically serves as the child's primary attachment figure.

This absorption of maternal behavior has long-term consequences. Once these foundational "programs" are in place, individuals often replay them throughout life, influencing their behaviours, emotional responses, and relationships. The learned patterns, especially in the context of anxiety, can lead to either adaptive or maladaptive outcomes depending on the nature of the environment to which the child is exposed.

Attachment Theory and Social Learning

Attachment theory, developed by John Bowlby and expanded by Mary Ainsworth (1978), emphasises the profound role that early interactions between a child and their primary caregiver play in shaping emotional security and personality. Bowlby posited that children form internal models of relationships based on the emotional availability and responsiveness of their caregivers, which affects how they perceive the world and approach relationships throughout their lives. Ainsworth's research on attachment styles, particularly through the Strange Situation experiment, highlighted how inconsistent caregiving from anxious mothers can lead to insecure attachments in children, which in turn fosters emotional instability and anxiety later in life.

Albert Bandura's social learning theory further underscores the role of environmental influences on behavior, suggesting that children learn through observation and imitation. When a mother consistently exhibits anxiety in response to stressors, children are likely to model this behavior, internalising it as the appropriate way to cope with challenges. Bandura's work demonstrates how these observed behaviours form the foundation for personality traits such as empathy, resilience, or, in the case of maternal anxiety, heightened stress responses.

Neuroscientific Insights

From a neuroscientific perspective, brain plasticity is at its peak during early childhood, meaning that a child's brain is particularly malleable and responsive to environmental stimuli. This plasticity allows for the rapid development of neural circuits that govern emotional regulation, empathy, and social behaviors. However, the same plasticity also means that children are highly sensitive to the emotional states of their caregivers, especially their mothers.

Research led by Dr. Jack Shonkoff (2000) of Harvard University's Centre on the Developing Child highlights that early life experiences play a critical role in shaping brain architecture. Positive environments, characterised by emotional warmth and secure attachments, support healthy brain development, whereas chronic stress or exposure to maternal anxiety can disrupt these neural circuits, increasing the risk of anxiety-related disorders.

Critical Developmental Windows

The vulnerability of children to maternal anxiety is especially pronounced during several key developmental windows. These "critical periods" are times when the brain is highly sensitive to external influences, making children particularly susceptible to absorbing and internalising the emotional climate of their home environment.

Infancy (0-2 Years)

In the first two years of life, a child's brain is undergoing rapid development, and their interactions with primary caregivers lay the groundwork for emotional and psychological growth. Infants are attuned to their caregivers' emotional states and depend on consistent, nurturing care to form secure attachments. When maternal anxiety disrupts this caregiving process, it can lead to insecure attachment styles, where the child struggles with emotional regulation and displays heightened stress responses.

Toddlerhood (2-5 Years)

During toddlerhood, children begin to develop a sense of independence and emotional awareness. However, they are still highly dependent on their mothers for emotional guidance. Anxious mothers may model stressful or fearful reactions to everyday challenges, inadvertently teaching their children that the world is a dangerous place. As a result, toddlers may exhibit excessive fearfulness, avoid new situations, and struggle with emotional regulation.

Early Childhood (5-7 Years)

By early childhood, children are forming more complex emotional and social skills. However, they are still vulnerable to the emotional states of their caregivers. Maternal anxiety during this period can lead children to interpret social interactions as threatening, withdraw from peers, or struggle with stress management. If these anxious behaviours are not addressed, they can become ingrained, increasing the risk of behavioural issues and anxiety disorders later in life.

Conclusion

The early years of life are marked by profound emotional, psychological, and neurobiological development. During these critical windows, children are particularly susceptible to absorbing parental anxiety, which can shape their long-term emotional health. By fostering secure attachments, modelling healthy emotional regulation, and creating a low-stress environment, caregivers can help children navigate these formative stages with confidence and emotional resilience. Addressing early signs of anxiety can prevent long-term emotional and behavioural issues, setting the stage for healthier development.

Chapter 17:

Maladaptive Attachment Types

Attachment Theory, pioneered by John Bowlby and later expanded by Mary Ainsworth (1978), provides a crucial framework for understanding how early emotional bonds with caregivers shape emotional regulation, interpersonal behavior, and overall psychological development. This chapter will explore the fundamental concepts of attachment theory, the different forms of attachment, and the long-term consequences of insecure attachment styles. We will also examine the maladaptive survival strategies that often emerge in adulthood as a result of early attachment experiences.

The Concept of Attachment

Attachment, as theorised by Bowlby, is an innate biological need for emotional security, formed primarily through the bond between a child and their caregiver. This emotional bond serves as a survival mechanism, ensuring the child's safety by fostering proximity to the caregiver, especially in stressful or dangerous situations. Children rely on their caregivers not only for physical protection but also for emotional regulation. The quality of these early attachment experiences shapes an individual's worldview, their emotional responses, and their interpersonal relationships throughout life. Bowlby emphasised that a child's early interactions with caregivers lay the foundation for their "internal working model"—a cognitive framework that informs their understanding of themselves, others, and relationships. A securely attached child sees the world as a safe place, trusts others, and develops a positive self-image. Conversely, insecure attachment can lead to distorted perceptions of self-worth and problematic interpersonal patterns.

Forms of Attachment

Secure Attachment

Characteristics: Securely attached children experience their caregivers as consistently available and responsive to their needs. They feel secure enough to explore their environment while trusting that their caregiver will be there if needed.

In Adulthood: Individuals with secure attachment tend to have healthy, balanced relationships. They are comfortable with intimacy, trust, and autonomy. Their positive internal working models enable them to cope with stress effectively and maintain supportive relationships.

Key Research: Ainsworth's Strange Situation study identified secure attachment behaviors, including children being distressed upon separation but easily comforted upon reunion with their caregiver.

Insecure-Avoidant Attachment

Characteristics: Children with avoidant attachment have learned that their caregiver is emotionally unavailable or dismissive. To protect themselves from the pain of rejection, these children minimise emotional expression and avoid seeking comfort.

In Adulthood: Avoidant individuals tend to avoid intimacy and rely on themselves emotionally. They may come across as emotionally distant or dismissive in relationships, often fearing vulnerability and preferring independence over close connections.

Key Research: Ainsworth observed that avoidant children exhibited minimal distress when their caregiver left and did not seek comfort upon their return, indicating emotional self-reliance and detachment.

Insecure-Ambivalent (Anxious) Attachment

Characteristics: Children with ambivalent attachment experience inconsistent caregiving. Their caregivers may sometimes be attentive but other times unavailable, leading the child to feel uncertain about the caregiver's reliability. As a result, these children become overly dependent and anxious about separation.

In Adulthood: Anxiously attached individuals often become preoccupied with relationships, fearing abandonment or rejection. They may exhibit clinginess, overdependence, or controlling behaviors as they strive to maintain emotional closeness.

Key Research: In the Strange Situation, ambivalent children were highly distressed when separated from their caregiver and had difficulty calming down, even when reunited.

Disorganised Attachment

Characteristics: Disorganised attachment arises when a child's caregiver is both a source of comfort and fear—often in cases of trauma, abuse, or neglect. The child does not develop a coherent strategy for dealing with emotional stress and may display contradictory behaviors.

In Adulthood: Adults with disorganised attachment struggle with trust and emotional regulation, often vacillating between extreme closeness and detachment in relationships. Their behaviors can be erratic, self-sabotaging, and rooted in unresolved trauma.

Key Research: Main and Solomon expanded Ainsworth's research by identifying disorganised attachment, observing children who appeared confused or fearful in the presence of their caregivers.

Maladaptive Survival Strategies in Adulthood

Attachment theory highlights how early attachment experiences with caregivers shape individuals' emotional regulation, coping strategies, and interpersonal behaviors throughout life. When caregivers are inconsistent, neglectful, or emotionally unavailable, children often develop insecure attachment styles—such as avoidant, ambivalent, or disorganised—that follow them into adulthood. These insecure attachment styles typically lead to maladaptive survival strategies, which individuals use to manage perceived threats in relationships, such as rejection, abandonment, or emotional harm. Although these strategies offer short-term relief, they reinforce negative patterns that complicate relationships and prevent emotional intimacy.

Avoidance as a Survival Strategy: Adults with avoidant attachment styles tend to maintain emotional distance in relationships. As children, they may have learned that their emotional needs would not be met consistently, prompting them to suppress vulnerability to avoid disappointment. In adulthood, they employ avoidance as a defence mechanism, avoiding deep emotional connections and difficult conversations. This creates a false sense of control and protection but also blocks intimacy and trust. For example, an individual with avoidant tendencies may disengage from conflicts or avoid expressing feelings, leaving their partner feeling emotionally disconnected.

Clinginess and Dependency: Anxiously attached adults often experience heightened fear of rejection and abandonment, leading them to seek constant reassurance and validation from their partners. As children, these individuals may have experienced inconsistent caregiving, making them unsure of their emotional security. As adults, they cope by becoming overly dependent or clingy, often resorting to behaviours such as jealousy or excessive checking on their partner to alleviate their fears. While this may provide temporary comfort, it creates relational strain, pushing partners away and reinforcing the anxiety that triggered the behavior in the first place.

Emotional Volatility: Disorganised attachment is often the result of trauma or severe inconsistency in early caregiving, leading to unpredictable and erratic behaviours in adulthood. Individuals with disorganised attachment vacillate between seeking closeness and pushing others away, creating instability in relationships. They may initiate conflicts or act in contradictory ways, driven by a fear of intimacy and trust issues. For instance, someone with disorganised attachment may act out by creating emotional distance, only to seek comfort and closeness soon after, perpetuating confusion and relational chaos.

Emotional Numbing: For individuals who experienced trauma or neglect, emotional numbing becomes a way to cope with vulnerability. By suppressing emotions, they protect themselves from potential hurt or rejection, but this comes at the cost of genuine connection. Emotional detachment often results in difficulty experiencing joy or empathy, further distancing them from loved ones. Though this strategy may have helped them survive emotionally in childhood, in adulthood, it prevents the formation of meaningful relationships.

The Cycle of Vulnerability & Survival Strategies

These maladaptive survival strategies often create a cycle of vulnerability in relationships. Fears of rejection, abandonment, or emotional harm trigger defensive behaviors such as avoidance, dependency, or emotional withdrawal.

These strategies, in turn, create barriers to authentic connection, trust, and emotional intimacy.

Critiques of Attachment Theory

Attachment theory, introduced by Bowlby and expanded by Ainsworth, has significantly influenced our understanding of early childhood development. However, critics argue that it overemphasises early experiences, implying that attachment styles rigidly dictate future emotional and social outcomes. Rutter (1981) and Lewis et al. (2000) challenged this deterministic view, highlighting the role of later relationships and life experiences in shaping emotional well-being. Kagan (1984) further criticised the theory for neglecting innate temperament, which may predispose children to specific attachment behaviors regardless of parental caregiving.

Cultural bias is another major critique, as attachment research largely reflects Western, individualistic societies. Takahashi (1990) and Keller (2018) argue that attachment classifications are not universally applicable, particularly in collectivist cultures where caregiving is shared. The Strange Situation experiment has also been criticised for lacking ecological validity, as it may not accurately capture attachment behaviors across diverse cultural contexts (Lamb et al., 1985). Additionally, the theory's focus on a primary caregiver (usually the mother) does not fully account for children raised by multiple caregivers (Rutter, 1995; Schaffer & Emerson, 1964).

Some critics contend that attachment theory pathologises insecurity, overlooking its potential adaptive functions. Ein-

Dor et al. (2010) and Fraley & Shaver (2000) suggest that anxious attachment can enhance vigilance in unpredictable environments. Pluess & Belsky (2010) highlight genetic influences, noting that sensitivity to caregiving varies among individuals. These critiques suggest that attachment is more fluid than originally proposed, warranting a broader, integrative approach.

Conclusion

Attachment theory offers valuable insights into how early relationships influence emotional development and shape interpersonal behaviors across the lifespan. Insecure attachment styles—such as avoidant, ambivalent, or disorganised—can contribute to maladaptive coping strategies in adulthood, potentially complicating relationships and reinforcing emotional vulnerability. While attachment theory has been widely studied, it has also faced criticism, particularly regarding its emphasis on early childhood experiences and cultural applicability. However, with self-awareness and therapeutic support, individuals can recognise these patterns, address attachment-related challenges, and foster healthier, more secure relationships in adulthood.

Part Six:

Family Dynamics

Chapter 18:

Intergenerational Family Dynamics

⟨ ❀ ⟩

This chapter examines the intricate family dynamics in households where both parents and grandparents experience anxiety, particularly within culturally diverse families navigating Western society. It explores the complex interplay of intergenerational anxiety shaped by traditional cultural expectations, Western parenting norms, and inherited anxiety behaviors that echo through generations. The chapter reveals how the tension between cultural heritage and adaptation to Western societal norms can compound anxiety, resulting in a nuanced, multilayered environment where both caregivers and children face emotional challenges.

Intergenerational Transmission of Anxiety

When both parents and grandparents exhibit anxious behaviors, children are often exposed to an environment where anxiety becomes a norm. Anxious grandparents may express concerns rooted in their traditional cultural frameworks, emphasising family honour, adherence to social norms, or rigid values (Rapee et al., 2009). These concerns are often inherited by parents who, while also managing Western pressures for child autonomy and self-expression, find themselves under dual pressure. This generational transmission often reinforces anxious behavior in children, as they internalise both cultural expectations from their grandparents and the adaptive stress responses from their mothers (Murray et al., 2009).

Studies show that children of anxious parents are at a heightened risk for anxiety disorders themselves, as they tend to adopt the coping mechanisms modelled by their primary caregivers (Bögels & Brechman-Toussaint, 2006). In families where grandparents and parents display anxious tendencies, children may experience what can be termed a "double reinforcement" effect. For instance, a grandmother's concerns over family reputation may combine with a mother's fears around social integration, resulting in compounded anxiety that encourages children to adopt avoidant and risk-averse behaviors. This intergenerational transmission not only affects the children's mental health but also establishes a family cycle of anxiety that can be difficult to break.

Cultural Dissonance and Parenting Conflicts

In families where cultural expectations from one generation meet Western norms, children and mothers often experience internal conflict. Grandparents from traditional backgrounds may value obedience, family loyalty, and adherence to cultural customs, while mothers, who aim to integrate their children into Western society, may lean toward fostering independence, critical thinking, and resilience (Kagitcibasi, 2007). This divergence can create tension between grandparents and parents as each tries to implement their respective parenting values, which may lead to inconsistent messaging and discipline strategies within the household.

For parents, balancing cultural expectations and Western societal pressures amplifies their anxiety, as they may feel pressured to protect their children from perceived threats in both cultural frameworks. The constant tension between respecting the elder generation's beliefs and adapting to new parenting strategies that prioritise a child's autonomy adds to maternal anxiety. This anxiety, in turn, influences children, who may internalise their mother's overprotectiveness or conflicting values, creating an environment where the child feels confused or insecure about their identity and expectations (Bögels & Phares, 2008).

Children's Emotional and Social Development

The emotional environment created by intergenerational anxiety can deeply affect children's development, particularly in emotional regulation and social interactions. Studies indicate that children raised in anxiety-laden environments often struggle with managing their own stress and may exhibit avoidance behaviors, perfectionism, or hypervigilance (Morris et al., 2007). Constant exposure to anxious behavior from primary caregivers makes it challenging for children to develop healthy emotional regulation, as they learn to interpret stress as an inevitable reaction to any uncertain situation.

Further, children raised amidst mixed cultural expectations often experience identity conflicts, feeling torn between the cultural values at home and the social norms they encounter outside. At school or with peers, they might be encouraged to be assertive and self-reliant, while at home, they could feel the pressure to respect family hierarchy and avoid behavior perceived as rebellious. This duality can lead to social isolation or reluctance to participate in activities that could conflict with family values, fostering a sense of detachment from both their cultural and social environments (Chen & Lee, 1996).

Emotions and Competing Expectations

Children growing up with competing expectations from extended families, parents, schools, peer groups, and society often feel a substantial emotional burden. Each group offers distinct values and standards, resulting in what could be termed a "push-pull" effect. For instance, grandparents may stress traditional customs and family loyalty, while parents may prioritise academic success or career achievements, and schools and peers may emphasise social adaptability and independence. Developmental psychologists like Bronfenbrenner, through his Ecological Systems Theory, emphasise that a child's development is highly influenced by these interacting environmental forces, particularly when expectations from these groups diverge (Bronfenbrenner, 1979).

The pressure to satisfy such varied expectations can lead to an emotional struggle, as children feel the need to "fit in" across different spheres of influence, which may be unrealistic and exhausting. Research highlights that such competing expectations increase stress, anxiety, and even contribute to identity confusion, as children feel caught between conforming to multiple ideals (Compas et al., 1993).

Positive and Negative Behavioural Responses

In the face of competing expectations, children may develop different coping mechanisms, which can either support or hinder their growth.

Positive Behavioural Responses

Adaptability and Resilience: Children who successfully navigate the push-pull effect of cultural and social expectations may develop strong adaptability, learning to adjust to diverse social norms. This skill fosters resilience, a valuable attribute in multicultural environments, as children learn to thrive amidst varying expectations (Masten, 2001).

Empathy and Cultural Awareness: Exposure to multiple viewpoints can enhance empathy and cultural sensitivity. These children become adept at understanding diverse perspectives, which fosters inclusivity and tolerance in a multicultural society, helping them build meaningful connections (Eisenberg & Strayer, 1987).

Independence and Critical Thinking: When children learn to manage differing expectations, they may develop critical thinking and independence. Feeling encouraged to make choices autonomously bolsters self-confidence and resilience, traits essential for navigating complex social environments (Eccles & Roeser, 2011).

Negative Behavioural Responses

Anxiety and Stress: The emotional strain of managing expectations can lead to increased anxiety and stress, as children may feel inadequate or pressured to conform to each group's standards. This stress, if unmanaged, can lead to psychological challenges (Compas et al., 1993).

Identity Confusion: Constantly adapting to different roles can result in identity confusion. Children may feel uncertain about their sense of self, particularly if they feel they are "performing" differently for each group, which can lead to issues in self-esteem and belonging (Erikson, 1968).

Rebellion or Withdrawal: In some instances, children may react by rebelling against cultural expectations or withdrawing from social interactions altogether to avoid the pressures imposed by family or society. This can hinder their social development and limit their ability to form stable relationships in the future (Steinberg, 2001).

Conclusion

Anxiety-related behaviors in extended families within diverse cultural contexts contribute significantly to family dynamics, influencing children's emotional resilience, adaptability, and sense of self. These children often grow up in environments where anxious behaviors are modelled and reinforced, creating a foundation for intergenerational anxiety.

Chapter 19:

Anxious Parents and Unfulfilled Dreams

In this chapter, we explore how anxious parents, driven by their own unmet needs and unresolved fears, may project their anxieties onto their children. These behaviours, often stemming from the parents fear of failure or the need for social validation, can lead to significant emotional and psychological burdens for children. We will explore these dynamics and their effects on child development through research evidence.

Projecting Unfulfilled Dreams onto Children

Anxious parents may unintentionally impose their unfulfilled dreams on their children, attempting to live vicariously through them. This pattern arises when parents, driven by their own disappointments or unmet goals, push their children to achieve the things they could not. Often, these parents believe that controlling their children's future will provide the emotional fulfillment they lack, not realising the damage it causes to their children's autonomy.

Diana Baumrind's research (1967) on parenting styles highlights the dangers of authoritarian parenting, where high demands are placed on children without considering their individual needs or desires. Children raised in such environments may develop anxiety, low self-esteem, or a lack of self-efficacy—the belief in their own ability to control their future.

Dr. Wendy Grolnick, in her research on controlling versus autonomy-supportive parenting, found that children of controlling parents often struggle with motivation and self-regulation. They may feel that their worth is tied to fulfilling their parents' expectations, leading to anxiety, guilt, and resentment.

Practical Impact on Children

Children who are pressured to fulfill their parents' unfulfilled dreams often feel that their personal desires are irrelevant, leading to feelings of helplessness or a lack of identity. Over time, they may struggle to understand their own passions or purpose, having lived in the shadow of their parent's ambitions. The constant pressure to achieve someone else's dreams can create emotional exhaustion and anxiety, as children feel they are never able to live up to their parent's expectations.

Using Children as Social Validation

In communities where competition between parents is high, anxious mothers may feel compelled to compete with other parents through their children's achievements. This competition is often driven by a need for social validation—the belief that their worth as a mother is measured by how well their children perform relative to their peers. In this scenario, children become instruments through which anxious mothers attempt to gain status or approval in their community, putting undue pressure on them to succeed academically, athletically, or socially.

Susan Harter's work on self-perception shows how parents' social comparisons—evaluating themselves against other parents—can lead to increased pressure on children. When children are used as status symbols, they are subject to high expectations and feel that their value is tied to their ability to bring pride to their parents, leading to chronic stress.

Edward Deci and Richard Ryan's Self-Determination Theory (2000) emphasises the importance of autonomy in child development. They argue that children who are pressured into achieving externally imposed goals (especially to satisfy parental needs for social comparison) are less likely to develop intrinsic motivation and may experience anxiety and depression due to a lack of autonomy.

Practical Impact on Children

Children who are used to compete in social status games often develop performance anxiety, fearing that any failure will result in disapproval or embarrassment for their parents. This pressure can lead to a cycle of overachievement, where the child constantly strives to meet unattainable standards, which in turn perpetuates anxiety and burnout.

The focus on external validation strips children of the joy of learning or achieving for themselves. Instead, they become externally motivated, working only to meet their parents' expectations or to win praise from others, often at the cost of their own happiness.

Helicopter Parenting and Overcontrol

Helicopter parenting refers to the tendency of some anxious mothers to be overly involved in their children's lives, micromanaging their daily activities and preventing them from making independent decisions. This behavior is often driven by the parents' fear that her child might fail or encounter harm if not constantly monitored. While this type of parenting may stem from a desire to protect the child, it often backfires, leading to issues with self-reliance and emotional regulation in the child.

Neil Montgomery (2010) found that children raised by helicopter parents often develop anxiety disorders or dependence issues, as they are not given the freedom to solve problems on their own. These children may struggle with making decisions, lack confidence, and feel anxious when faced with challenges because they have not been allowed to fail or learn from mistakes.

Annette Lareau's research (2003) on parenting styles emphasises the dangers of concerted cultivation—a form of overparenting where parents orchestrate every aspect of their child's life. While these children may excel in structured environments, they often lack the resilience to cope with adversity or unexpected changes.

Practical Impact on Children

Children of helicopter parents may not develop the ability to cope with challenges independently. They may become overly reliant on their parents for decision-making and struggle to navigate life's uncertainties without parental guidance.

Constant supervision and intervention send a message to children that failure is unacceptable, fostering a fear of taking risks or trying new things, which limits their personal growth and development.

Parental Expectations in Career Choices

Anxious parents may also select careers for their children, disregarding their children's personal interests or abilities. Driven by their own fears or desires for stability and success, these mothers may push their children into fields that promise financial security or social prestige, even if the child's passions lie elsewhere. This type of overcontrol can stifle the child's creativity, curiosity, and intrinsic motivation, leading to long-term dissatisfaction and anxiety.

I acknowledge the importance of parents' role (rights) in guiding their children's educational and career paths. However, a balanced approach, which incorporates the child's own wishes, opinions, and expectations, can lead to more collaborative and fulfilling decision-making. By considering the child's perspective, parents can foster a dialogue that respects both guidance and individuality.

Laurence Steinberg's research (1967) on parental influence suggests that parents who overly direct their child's career choices can undermine their child's identity formation and sense of self. When children are forced into careers they did not choose, they may develop resentment and anxiety, particularly if they feel trapped in a path they cannot escape. Richard Ryan and Edward Deci's Self-Determination Theory (2000) also applies here, as it posits that individuals must have autonomy to thrive. Children who are pressured into specific careers by their parents may struggle with intrinsic motivation and job satisfaction, which increases the likelihood of burnout and mental health issues later in life.

Practical Impact on Children

Diminished passion and fulfillment: Children pushed into careers they did not choose are more likely to feel unfulfilled and may struggle to find meaning in their work. This lack of personal connection to their career can lead to chronic stress, disengagement, and emotional exhaustion.

Children who feel their parents controlled their career paths may develop feelings of resentment toward their parents, leading to strained relationships and emotional distancing. In some cases, this can result in rebellion, where the child eventually rejects the parent's choices, even if doing so leads to conflict.

The Emotional Toll of Parental Pressure

When anxious parents impose their own dreams, control, and expectations on their children, they risk making their children's lives emotionally draining and miserable. Children who feel constantly pressured to meet their parents' demands may internalise feelings of inadequacy, fear, and resentment, which can manifest as anxiety, depression, or self-esteem issues.

Julie Lythcott-Haims (2015), in her book How to Raise an Adult, discusses how overparenting and pressuring children can lead to mental health issues. Children raised under constant pressure may suffer from perfectionism, high anxiety, and a fear of failure, which can persist into adulthood.

Dr. Suniya Luthar's research on children of affluent families (2005, 2012) shows that overpressure from parents can lead to substance abuse, mental health disorders, and behavioural issues as children attempt to cope with unrealistic expectations.

Practical Impact on Children

The relentless pressure to meet parental expectations can leave children feeling emotionally drained, especially when they feel their own desires and interests are disregarded. The constant stress of trying to please their parents, combined with the fear of failure, can result in chronic anxiety and depression. Children may also feel a sense of hopelessness, believing that they can never meet their parents' expectations.

Conclusion

In this chapter, we explored how anxious parents, driven by their own unmet needs and fears of failure, may project these anxieties onto their children. By trying to fulfill their own unfulfilled dreams or compete with other parents, they inadvertently burden their children with unrealistic expectations, causing emotional strain, loss of autonomy, and chronic anxiety. The breaking the cycle is challenging.

Chapter 20:

Relationship Breakdown and

Anxiety

———— ◯ ⁂ ◯ ————

This chapter examines how ongoing and unresolved anxiety can profoundly impact adult relationships, often contributing to marital and relationship breakdowns. Difficulty with emotional regulation, trust, and intimacy can create a cycle of conflict, withdrawal, and instability between partners. These relational struggles extend beyond the couple, affecting children by exposing them to chronic stress, inconsistent caregiving, and emotional turbulence. Growing up in an environment marked by anxiety-driven conflict can heighten a child's own anxiety levels, disrupt their sense of security, and influence their ability to form healthy relationships in the future.

Emotional Dysregulation and Marital Conflict

Research shows that individuals with anxiety often experience heightened emotional reactivity, making it challenging to manage daily stress calmly (Aldao et al., 2010). Within a marriage, this heightened reactivity can result in increased misunderstandings and conflicts. For instance, an anxious partner may misinterpret neutral comments or actions as criticisms, prompting defensive or confrontational behaviors. Over time, these recurring misunderstandings can create a cycle of negativity that erodes emotional intimacy and marital satisfaction (Fincham & Beach, 2010).

When one or both partners struggle to regulate negative emotions, minor disagreements can escalate into significant conflicts. Anxiety often leads individuals to overanalyse situations, catastrophise outcomes, or respond impulsively, intensifying relational tensions. Such dynamics can erode the foundation of trust and mutual respect in a relationship, leaving both partners feeling emotionally drained and unsupported. This decline in marital quality is further compounded by unresolved conflicts, fostering dissatisfaction and resentment.

Anxiety's Impact on Trust and Intimacy

Anxiety disorders have a profound impact on trust and intimacy, the pillars of a healthy relationship. Individuals with anxiety may fear judgment or rejection, making it difficult to openly share thoughts and vulnerabilities with their partner (Greenberg & Goldman, 2008). This reluctance to communicate fosters emotional distance, leaving the other partner feeling excluded or disconnected. Over time, this lack of openness undermines the emotional bond that sustains a marriage.

Moreover, anxious individuals often adopt compensatory behaviors, such as excessive people-pleasing or withdrawal, to cope with their fears. These extremes can create imbalance and strain in the relationship. For example, if an anxious partner avoids discussing their struggles, the other partner may feel neglected or undervalued, further deepening the emotional divide (Brené Brown, 2012).

Anxiety-Driven Behaviors & Validation-Seeking

Anxiety often manifests in maladaptive survival strategies, such as seeking constant validation or becoming overly self-critical. While these behaviors aim to reduce uncertainty, they can strain relationships. For instance, an anxious parent seeking excessive reassurance from their partner may inadvertently cause emotional fatigue, leading to withdrawal. Brené Brown's work on vulnerability and shame illustrates how anxiety can drive behaviors like perfectionism, blame, or emotional detachment, which erode intimacy and trust over time. These patterns often perpetuate cycles of emotional instability in children, extending anxiety's influence across generations (Brown, 2012).

The Legacy of Broken Families

Parents from broken families—where divorce, separation, or absent caregivers were prevalent—often carry unresolved feelings of insecurity into adulthood. Exposure to family violence during childhood further compounds this anxiety, shaping expectations of relationships as inherently unstable or unsafe (Tronick, 1978). These early experiences influence emotional regulation and attachment patterns, making it challenging to form secure, healthy adult relationships.

The Still-Face Paradigm (Tronick, 1978) highlights how disruptions in parental responsiveness during early life can exacerbate emotional insecurity. This insecurity often leads to hypervigilance and heightened anxiety in adult relationships, where individuals remain on constant alert for perceived threats.

Romantic and Physical Relationships

Anxiety significantly impacts romantic and physical relationships, often creating distance between partners. Chronic stress and caregiving demands can lead to emotional exhaustion, leaving anxious parents with limited capacity for intimacy. Stress hormones like cortisol interfere with the body's production of oxytocin and other bonding hormones, reducing closeness and affection (Carter, 1998).

For anxious partners, emotional withdrawal or sensitivity to criticism may further complicate romantic dynamics, creating barriers to intimacy. These challenges can perpetuate feelings of disconnection and dissatisfaction, contributing to marital breakdowns.

Panic Disorder and Intimacy

The study Marriage in a Panic: Panic Disorder and Intimate Relationships (Kasalova et al. 2020) highlights the significant impact of panic disorder on marital relationships. Panic symptoms often lead to increased conflicts and communication breakdowns, creating a negative cycle that exacerbates both the disorder and relational difficulties. Unresolved conflicts within the marriage are identified as a major predictor of symptom relapses, with chronic stress in the relationship worsening mental health outcomes for the affected partner. Additionally, partner dissatisfaction during therapy is linked to less successful treatment, emphasising the importance of addressing marital dynamics alongside individual therapy to support better outcomes.

The study also explores the complex relationship between panic disorder and fears of abandonment, noting a cyclical interplay that can destabilise both the individual and the marriage. It suggests that couples therapy may be instrumental in addressing both relational conflicts and the psychological aspects of panic disorder. Overall, the findings underscore the need to incorporate the marital context into treatment plans, as the quality of the relationship significantly influences the success of therapy and the individual's recovery.

Emotional Instability and Marital Breakdown

Parents with unresolved anxiety may exhibit heightened sensitivity, misinterpreting neutral behaviors from their partner as threats. This hypervigilance often leads to emotional volatility, which can escalate conflict within a marriage. In some cases, maternal anxiety manifests as overprotectiveness or controlling behavior, straining the marital dynamic and stifling healthy communication.

When marriages break down due to parental anxiety, children often internalise feelings of abandonment, deepening their vulnerability to anxiety. Studies on Adverse Childhood Experiences (ACEs) highlight that exposure to family conflict or instability significantly increases the likelihood of anxiety disorders and emotional dysregulation in adulthood (Felitti et al., 1998).

The Bidirectional Cycle of Anxiety

Parental anxiety both causes and results from family breakdowns, creating a bidirectional cycle. Anxious parents may unintentionally contribute to dysfunctional dynamics, such as conflict or emotional withdrawal, which destabilise relationships. In turn, these dynamics create environments where children are more likely to develop anxiety disorders, perpetuating the cycle.

Conclusion

This chapter has examined how unresolved parental anxiety can strain relationships, contributing to marital breakdowns and ongoing family disputes. Anxiety can manifest in patterns of emotional withdrawal, excessive control, or heightened conflict, creating an unstable family environment. When parents struggle with anxiety-driven tensions, children are often caught in the middle, exposed to unpredictable emotional climates and inconsistent caregiving. The breakdown of family structures can intensify a child's own anxiety, affecting their emotional security, stress regulation, and ability to form trusting relationships. Research suggests that children from high-conflict or separated families may develop heightened sensitivity to stress, an increased risk of attachment difficulties, and a greater likelihood of experiencing anxiety disorders later in life.

Chapter 21:

Family Violence and Impact on Children

<hr>

Family violence is a pervasive issue with profound and far-reaching consequences for children's emotional development, mental health, and overall well-being. Defined as abuse—whether physical, emotional, sexual, psychological, or neglectful—occurring within familial or intimate relationships, family violence creates a toxic environment that fundamentally disrupts children's sense of safety and security.

Emotional and Psychological Impact on Children

According to the World Health Organisation (2021), one in three women globally experiences physical or sexual violence, often perpetrated by an intimate partner. However, children, elderly parents, and men are also vulnerable to various forms of family violence, highlighting its complex and multifaceted nature. The effects of family violence are profound, shaping emotional regulation, attachment patterns, and behavioural development while perpetuating a cycle of trauma and dysfunction across generations.

Children exposed to family violence often exhibit heightened anxiety, depression, emotional dysregulation, and post-traumatic stress disorder (PTSD). Kitzmann et al. (2003) found that 63% of children who witnessed domestic violence displayed significant emotional or behavioural issues, compared to 35% in non-exposed children. Repeated exposure to violence sensitises children to stress, impairing their ability to regulate emotions and increasing hypervigilance to perceived threats. This chronic anxiety can lead to difficulty in managing fear and worry, resulting in persistent emotional instability. Margolin and Vickerman (2007) emphasised how children adopt maladaptive coping strategies, such as aggression or withdrawal, as mechanisms to manage the ongoing fear and distress associated with living in violent households.

Evans et al. (2008) further emphasised that childhood exposure to intimate partner violence (IPV) predicts heightened symptoms of generalised anxiety and PTSD in later life. Behaviourally, Herrenkohl et al. (2008) found that children in violent homes often display increased aggression and antisocial tendencies, which can persist into adulthood.

Impact on Adults

Adults exposed to family violence during childhood or adulthood are vulnerable to severe mental and physical health consequences. Studies such as Bonomi et al. (2006) and Carbone-López et al. (2006) found that individuals exposed to IPV as children are more likely to develop PTSD, with symptoms reported in 50% of IPV-exposed women compared to 13% in non-exposed groups. The Adverse Childhood Experiences (ACE) Study (Felitti et al., 1998) established strong connections between childhood violence exposure and chronic illnesses like cardiovascular disease, diabetes, and autoimmune disorders. Additionally, Coker et al. (2002) reinforced that IPV-exposed women frequently report chronic pain, gastrointestinal issues, and reproductive health problems. Substance abuse is another significant consequence, with Widom et al. (2007) and Dube et al. (2002) finding that individuals exposed to family violence are 2–4 times more likely to develop substance use disorders as a way of coping with unresolved trauma.

Developmental and Cognitive Consequences

Family violence disrupts crucial developmental processes, particularly in forming secure attachments. Bowlby's attachment theory underscores the role of stable caregiver relationships in fostering emotional security. However, children in violent homes frequently develop insecure attachments marked by fear, instability, or distrust. These attachment disruptions often impair their ability to form healthy relationships in adulthood, perpetuating cycles of emotional dysfunction. Cognitive development is also at risk. Prolonged exposure to violence affects key brain structures like the hippocampus and amygdala, which are essential for memory and emotional regulation. Studies by Evans et al. (2008) reveal that children exposed to intimate partner violence are more likely to develop symptoms of PTSD and anxiety during adolescence and adulthood, suggesting that the impact of early trauma extends far beyond childhood.

The Psychological Roots of Sexual Abuse

The psychological roots of sexual abuse often originate from early developmental experiences, including attachment disruptions, trauma, and adverse childhood environments. Individuals with insecure or disorganised attachment histories, shaped by neglect, inconsistent caregiving, or family dysfunction, may develop emotional dysregulation, low self-worth, and a poor understanding of boundaries. These challenges, compounded by unmet needs for intimacy or control, increase the vulnerability to maladaptive behaviors, including sexually abusive actions. Early relational experiences play a critical role in forming healthy interpersonal connections, and disruptions during this phase can lead to significant social and emotional deficits.

Trauma, particularly the intergenerational transmission of abuse, is a significant factor in the psychology of sexual abuse. Perpetrators often have personal histories of physical, emotional, or sexual abuse, which distort their perceptions of relationships and normalise exploitative behavior. Unresolved trauma can drive maladaptive coping mechanisms, such as using power and control to manage feelings of insecurity or inadequacy. Early exposure to violence or sexual exploitation increases the likelihood of perpetuating abusive behavior, as individuals struggle to process and heal from their trauma in healthy ways.

Cognitive distortions and empathy deficits further contribute to the psychological roots of sexual abuse. Perpetrators often justify their actions through distorted beliefs, minimise harm, or blame their victims, enabling them to evade accountability. A lack of empathy, often rooted in attachment disruptions, impairs their ability to understand or respect others' feelings and boundaries. These deficits, coupled with emotional immaturity or antisocial tendencies, increase the likelihood of exploitation. Addressing these psychological roots through targeted interventions is critical for breaking the cycle of abuse and fostering healthier, prosocial behavioural patterns.

Behavioural Implications

Children in violent homes often exhibit externalising behaviors such as aggression, defiance, and antisocial tendencies. These behaviors are learned responses to chaotic environments and reflect an attempt to regain control or express emotional distress. Herrenkohl et al. (2008) demonstrated that such behaviors often lead to difficulties in academic settings, strained peer relationships, and increased risks of delinquent behavior in adolescence and adulthood. Over time, these behavioural issues can entrench patterns of instability and maladaptive coping mechanisms, creating challenges in social and interpersonal functioning.

Multigenerational Transmission of Trauma

Family violence often perpetuates a multigenerational cycle of trauma and emotional dysregulation. Parents who fail to address their own unresolved anxieties or traumatic experiences may unconsciously project these onto their children, fostering emotional instability. This dynamic can result in insecure attachments, heightened vulnerability to mental health challenges, and the replication of maladaptive behaviors in future relationships. Widom et al. (2007) highlighted how unresolved childhood trauma increases susceptibility to substance abuse, unstable relationships, and mental health disorders in adulthood, emphasising the need for early interventions to disrupt this cycle.

Conclusion

Family violence disrupts children's emotional and cognitive development, fostering anxiety, trauma, and behavioural challenges that can persist into adulthood. The impacts are deeply ingrained, influencing attachment patterns, emotional regulation, and social functioning, and perpetuating cycles of dysfunction. Breaking this cycle requires a comprehensive approach that addresses the root causes of violence, supports victims, and promotes resilience through early intervention and systemic change. By prioritising targeted support for children and families, society can mitigate the profound effects of family violence and ensure healthier outcomes for future generations.

Part Seven:

Breaking the Cycle and Prospects

Chapter 22:

Natural Healing Process of

Anxiety

———— ❧ ————

This chapter highlights the natural healing mechanisms that follow every "fight or flight" response, illustrating how the body strives to restore balance after episodes of anxiety or stress. By recognising and strengthening these innate processes, individuals can maintain emotional equilibrium more effectively from the outset. This chapter outlines the body's intrinsic ability to recover from anxiety, offering practical strategies that help parents enhance their natural healing response. By tapping into these mechanisms, parents can foster a more stable emotional environment, benefiting both themselves and their families.

Anxiety as a Natural Safety Program

As explored in previous chapters, anxiety can be seen as a natural safety mechanism, or "safety program," that has evolved to protect us from potential threats. Originating from our ancient ancestors, anxiety functioned as an adaptive survival response: it prepared the body to recognise, react to, and avoid dangers in the environment. This survival response, commonly referred to as the "fight-or-flight" response, involves a release of hormones like adrenaline and cortisol, which enhance alertness and prepare the body for action. In this way, anxiety primes us to either confront or evade perceived threats, helping us survive immediate dangers and develop strategies to avoid similar threats in the future. We already discovered that while this "safety program" continues to serve a purpose by alerting us to challenges and promoting cautious behavior, its overactivation can lead to a persistent state of heightened alertness and stress. Understanding anxiety as a natural, albeit sometimes overly-sensitive, protective response can help in managing it, enabling us to leverage its benefits while learning strategies to keep it from interfering with daily

The Body's Natural Healing Process

The healing process from stress and anxiety is rooted in the body's autonomic nervous system (ANS), which regulates physiological responses to perceived threats. The ANS comprises two key branches: the sympathetic nervous system (SNS) and the parasympathetic nervous system (PNS). The SNS triggers the fight-or-flight response when the brain perceives a threat, preparing the body to either confront or flee from danger. In contrast, the PNS, often referred to as the "rest-and-digest" system, helps restore balance once the threat has subsided.

When faced with stress, the amygdala, the brain's emotional processing centre, activates the hypothalamus, which signals the adrenal glands to release stress hormones like cortisol and adrenaline. These hormones increase heart rate, elevate blood pressure, and divert energy to muscles, preparing the body for immediate action. This response was crucial for our ancestors' survival, helping them escape predators or other physical dangers.

Once the threat is neutralised, the body engages the parasympathetic nervous system to restore balance or return to Homeostasis. The PNS slows the heart rate, lowers blood pressure, and redirects energy to digestion, immune function, and relaxation. This natural healing process is essential for recovery, allowing the body and mind to reset after the heightened state of arousal caused by the fight-or-flight response.

Enhance the Healing Process

Enhancing the natural healing process for anxiety involves approaches that support the body and mind's ability to calm itself, return to balance, and reset after stress. Here are key methods that support this natural healing:

1. Physical Grounding Techniques

Deep Breathing: Controlled breathing techniques like diaphragmatic or "belly" breathing help activate the parasympathetic nervous system, which counters anxiety by slowing down the heart rate and reducing cortisol levels. Practicing this for a few minutes daily can significantly decrease symptoms of anxiety. Breathe in deeply through your nose for a count of four, hold the breath for four, and then exhale slowly through your mouth for a count of six or eight. Repeat this cycle several times to engage and activate parasympathetic nervous system.

Progressive Muscle Relaxation (PMR): In PMR, you systematically tense and release muscle groups throughout the body. This approach not only releases physical tension but also reinforces awareness of where stress is held in the body, promoting relaxation.

Movement and Exercise: Physical activity releases endorphins, which help regulate mood. Gentle activities like yoga or stretching also reduce physical tension while positively influencing emotional states.

2. Building Positive Lifestyle Habits

Adequate Sleep: Poor sleep and anxiety are closely linked. Regular sleep patterns enhance brain function and emotional regulation, while reducing anxiety symptoms. Avoiding caffeine close to bedtime and maintaining a consistent sleep schedule can improve sleep quality.

Balanced Nutrition: Nutrients like magnesium, omega-3 fatty acids, and complex carbohydrates can stabilise mood and promote relaxation. Avoiding processed foods and consuming a balanced diet supports brain function and emotional health.

Hydration and Limiting Stimulants: Proper hydration helps in reducing cortisol levels. Limiting caffeine and other stimulants can prevent heightened anxiety, as these substances often worsen symptoms.

3. Social and Relational Support

Social Connection: Engaging in meaningful social interactions can release oxytocin, a hormone that promotes feelings of safety and reduces stress responses. Spending time with friends or loved ones creates a support network, buffering against the effects of anxiety.

Support Groups or Counselling: Talking to others facing similar challenges provides emotional relief and offers strategies for coping. Therapy, including techniques like EMDR and hypnotherapy, may also support natural healing when anxiety has roots in unresolved trauma.

By integrating these practices, individuals can enhance the body's ability to manage and reduce anxiety naturally, gradually building resilience and a stronger foundation for emotional well-being

Theories Supporting Natural Recovery

Polyvagal Theory

Dr. Stephen Porges' Polyvagal Theory (2011) emphasises the role of the vagus nerve in managing stress and promoting emotional regulation. Enhancing the function of the polyvagal nerve, or vagus nerve, can promote relaxation, emotional regulation, and overall resilience to stress. The polyvagal theory, developed by Dr. Stephen Porges, emphasises the importance of the vagus nerve in controlling the parasympathetic nervous system, which is responsible for the "rest-and-digest" response. By stimulating the vagus nerve, individuals can activate the calming and restorative functions of the body, improving their ability to cope with stress and anxiety. Here are several other techniques to enhance the polyvagal nerve:

1. Cold Exposure: Exposure to cold can activate the vagus nerve and improve vagal tone, which helps in regulating stress responses. Cold exposure stimulates the vagus nerve and can lead to increased parasympathetic activity. Taking cold showers or splashing cold water on your face for 30 seconds to a minute is an easy way to stimulate the vagus nerve.

2. Humming or Chanting: The vagus nerve is connected to the vocal cords and the muscles at the back of the throat. Humming, singing, or chanting can help activate the vagus nerve and increase parasympathetic activity. Humming or chanting regularly, especially during meditation or deep breathing exercises, can enhance vagal tone. Singing in groups or even softly to yourself has been shown to have positive effects on the vagus nerve.

3. Gargling: Gargling stimulates the muscles in the throat, which are connected to the vagus nerve. This simple exercise can help improve vagal tone. Gargle with water for 30 seconds to a minute every day to stimulate the vagus nerve.

4. Yoga and Tai Chi: These mind-body practices, which emphasise breath control and gentle movements, are known to stimulate the vagus nerve and promote relaxation. Regular practice of yoga or Tai Chi can help activate the vagus nerve by incorporating deep breathing, meditation, and mindful movement.

5. Mindfulness Meditation: Mindfulness meditation practices have been shown to improve vagal tone by promoting relaxation and reducing the fight-or-flight response. Engage in mindfulness or loving-kindness meditation by focusing on the present moment, deep breathing, and cultivating feelings of compassion. Even a few minutes of mindfulness practice each day can help stimulate the vagus nerve.

6. Social Engagement: According to the polyvagal theory, positive social interactions can stimulate the vagus nerve. Engaging in meaningful connections, maintaining eye contact, and showing empathy help increase parasympathetic activity. Spend time with loved ones, engage in active listening, and practice eye contact during conversations to promote vagal tone through social connection.

7. Massage: Neck or abdominal massage can stimulate the vagus nerve and promote relaxation. Gently massaging the carotid sinus (located in the neck) or practicing abdominal massage can activate the vagus nerve and calm the body.

These techniques, when practiced regularly, can help enhance the polyvagal nerve's function and improve stress resilience. Developing strong vagal tone is crucial for overall emotional and physical well-being, making it easier for individuals to shift from states of stress to calm.

Other Notable Strategies

In "Overcoming Parental Anxiety," (Kissen, D; Ioffe, M & Romain, H. 2022), several effective strategies are outlined to help parents manage their own anxiety, which can positively impact their well-being and their child's emotional health. The following four strategies from their list appear useful.

Self-care is foundational to this approach. While often misunderstood as a luxury or indulgence, the authors clarify that true self-care involves consistent attention to one's mental and emotional needs. This might include setting aside time for personal hobbies, regular physical activity, or seeking therapy. By making self-care a priority, parents can cultivate the resilience needed to navigate the demands of parenting. This, in turn, allows them to support their children more effectively, fostering a positive, balanced family environment.

Another strategy is practicing **self-compassion**. Many parents tend to be their harshest critics, especially when they feel they've fallen short. The book encourages shifting this mindset by adopting a more compassionate, understanding approach to self-talk. Instead of dwelling on perceived shortcomings, parents are urged to treat themselves with kindness, much like they would a friend. This inner gentleness helps to reduce guilt and self-doubt, alleviating the anxiety that often accompanies high self-expectations. Embracing self-compassion enables parents to address daily challenges with a clearer, more composed mindset, which benefits both them and their children.

Another critical aspect highlighted is the importance of developing **trust in one's child**. Recognising the natural limits of control and allowing children to experience challenges fosters resilience and self-confidence. Rather than attempting to shield children from every difficulty, parents are encouraged to support their children's independence, thereby reducing their own anxiety and enabling their children to develop effective coping skills.

Lastly, **modelling calmness** is presented as an invaluable tool. Children often mirror their parents' emotional reactions, so the way parents handle stress can significantly shape a child's own responses to anxiety. By modelling calmness, parents create a stable emotional environment that helps children learn to navigate their own feelings constructively. Observing calm, resilient behaviors in their parents gives children a reliable blueprint for managing their own stress.

These strategies are designed to be integrative, offering parents a framework for building a more balanced and fulfilling approach to both parenting and self-care. Over time, these practices not only enhance the parents' mental well-being but also provide a foundation for children to develop their resilience and emotional intelligence, equipping them to manage anxiety and face life's challenges with confidence.

Conclusion

For anxious parents, awareness is the first step toward healing. By understanding how their body naturally processes stress and learning to engage the parasympathetic response, they can actively reduce anxiety and create a more peaceful environment for themselves and their families. Healing from anxiety is not a one-time event but an ongoing process of self-awareness, emotional regulation, and deliberate action. With the right strategies—such as mindfulness, deep breathing, polyvagal nerve enhancing, social support, and emotional resilience training—mothers can break the cycle of anxiety and foster a sense of calm and security in their homes. By prioritising their mental health, they not only enhance their well-being but also model healthy coping mechanisms for their children, laying the foundation for a more emotionally balanced future.

Chapter 23:

Deliberate Actions to Overcome Anxiety

―――――― ◯ ⚜ ◯ ――――――

This chapter highlights the importance of deliberate actions to address anxiety when natural healing mechanisms alone are insufficient. While the body's innate ability to manage stress and anxiety is powerful, there are times when additional support is essential—particularly for parents coping with chronic anxiety. This chapter serves as a guide to managing anxiety through formal therapeutic approaches that extend beyond natural recovery. Among the wide range of therapeutic methods available, this chapter focuses on a selection of key approaches, offering readers insights into effective strategies for addressing anxiety in a more targeted and structured manner.

Understanding the Need for Deliberate Action

An anxious parent may often struggle with discerning real threats from perceived ones due to the heightened emotional responses that anxiety triggers. If the natural state of healing (where the body activates its parasympathetic nervous system after stress) does not bring relief, it's crucial to engage in deliberate steps to manage the anxiety. Chronic anxiety can become self-perpetuating, blurring the line between genuine concerns and exaggerated fears, making it essential to identify when outside intervention is needed.

As already established in this publication, the body's fight-or-flight mechanism is meant to protect us in moments of acute stress. However, when this state is prolonged, it becomes harmful. Chronic activation of the stress response can lead to physical health issues like cardiovascular problems, cognitive impairments, and emotional instability. This is where deliberate interventions—both psychological and physiological—become critical to breaking the cycle of stress and anxiety.

When self-regulation and self-care strategies fall short, deliberate therapy offers structured support to help parents manage and mitigate anxiety. Several models have proven to be effective in addressing maternal anxiety. They are briefly introduced below.

Evolutionary Psychology-based Approaches

Evolutionary psychology provides unique insights into anxiety, framing it as an adaptive mechanism shaped by natural selection to protect against threats. Therapy approaches grounded in this perspective aim to recalibrate overactive survival mechanisms to better align with modern contexts. Below are four key therapy approaches based on evolutionary principles.

1. Exposure Therapy: Retraining Threat Responses

Exposure therapy leverages the evolutionary understanding that anxiety arises from hypervigilance and overgeneralised threat responses, evolved to prioritise caution. While avoidance behaviors provide immediate relief, they reinforce the brain's perception of danger, perpetuating the anxiety cycle. Exposure therapy gradually and repeatedly introduces clients to feared stimuli, allowing the brain to recalibrate its threat-detection system as the perceived danger proves to be harmless. For example, a person with social anxiety may start by engaging in small, low-stakes interactions and progressively work up to more challenging social situations. This approach is highly effective for phobias, PTSD, and panic disorders, helping individuals reduce their fear responses over time by reconditioning their brain to tolerate and eventually diminish the fear.

2. Reframing Anxiety Through Psychoeducation

Psychoeducation grounded in evolutionary psychology reframes anxiety as a natural byproduct of the brain's adaptive "smoke detector" mechanism, designed to err on the side of caution. Educating clients about this evolutionary origin reduces stigma, self-blame, and fear of their symptoms. Therapists explain how anxiety evolved to protect against potential threats, even though it often generates false alarms in modern, low-risk environments. Using metaphors like the "overactive smoke detector," therapists help clients view their symptoms as normal but exaggerated responses. For instance, explaining that panic attacks are the body's way of preparing for danger—not a sign of physical illness or personal failure—can significantly reduce symptom-related anxiety. This approach enhances clients' understanding of their condition, increases self-compassion, and improves their engagement in therapy.

3. Mindfulness & Acceptance-Based Interventions

Mindfulness and acceptance-based interventions capitalise on the brain's evolved capacity to monitor internal states and regulate attention, helping reduce overactivation of the amygdala and other anxiety-related neural pathways. These approaches encourage clients to observe their anxiety without judgment, breaking the feedback loop of escalating fear. Acceptance and Commitment Therapy (ACT) (Hayes, et al. 2012)., for example, integrates mindfulness practices with strategies to accept anxiety as a natural response while focusing on living a value-driven life. Instead of resisting or suppressing anxiety, clients learn to acknowledge and coexist with it. A person with generalised anxiety might use mindfulness techniques, such as focused breathing or body scans, to ground themselves during moments of worry, allowing them to detach from the fear and redirect their attention to meaningful actions. These interventions are particularly effective for generalised anxiety disorder, social anxiety, and stress-related conditions.

4. Lifestyle Aligned with Ancestral Needs

Lifestyle interventions address the mismatch between modern living and the ancestral environments to which human physiology and psychology are adapted. Anxiety often stems from chronic stressors that deviate from the natural rhythms of early human life, such as sedentary lifestyles, social isolation, and overstimulation. Encouraging clients to engage in regular physical exercise, maintain consistent sleep hygiene, spend time in natural environments, and foster supportive social connections can significantly reduce anxiety. For example, a therapist might recommend daily walks in nature and participation in community groups to counteract modern stressors and align with evolutionary adaptations for stress regulation. By addressing systemic contributors to anxiety, lifestyle interventions improve overall mental health and provide a sustainable foundation for long-term recovery.

Other models

Cognitive-Behavioural Therapy (CBT)

Cognitive-Behavioural Therapy (CBT) is a professional therapeutic approach highly effective for managing anxiety, including maternal anxiety. CBT is based on evolutionary psychology principals. CBT operates on the understanding that anxious thoughts and behaviors are interlinked and that altering maladaptive thoughts can significantly reduce anxiety symptoms. In therapy, individuals are guided to recognise and challenge irrational or exaggerated thoughts, such as fearing the worst-case scenario in everyday situations. For example, an anxious mother worried about her child's health can learn to assess whether her fears are grounded in evidence or are catastrophising. This process of reframing fears helps her to see situations more realistically, reducing anxiety's impact on her behavior and interactions with her child.

CBT involves specific techniques, including cognitive restructuring, automatic though records, decataspropising, behavioural activation, activity scheduling, and behavioural experiments, that help individuals transform negative thought patterns into more constructive perspectives. Cognitive restructuring is central to CBT and encourages clients to question the validity of their worries. For example, an anxious parent might learn to shift from "My child will certainly get sick" to "There are ways I can help keep my child healthy." This cognitive shift allows individuals to manage anxiety without resorting to avoidance or control behaviors. Behavioural experiments are another effective CBT tool that tests the accuracy of one's beliefs, helping clients gradually face their fears in manageable steps, which builds confidence and reduces anxiety over time.

In addition to cognitive tools, CBT often incorporates mindfulness practices to foster present-moment awareness, which helps individuals observe thoughts and emotions without judgment. Regular mindfulness practice has been shown to alter the brain's response to stress, enhancing emotional resilience. CBT's structured approach and emphasis on self-reflection through techniques like journaling also encourage individuals to record and process their fears, turning their focus from anxieties to positive aspects of life. By reducing the frequency and intensity of negative thoughts, CBT provides a framework for managing anxiety sustainably, empowering individuals to navigate their fears with greater confidence and emotional balance.

Attachment-Based Therapy

Attachment-based therapy is rooted in attachment theory, which underscores the vital role of early relationships in shaping emotional health, resilience, and overall psychological well-being. Attachment theory, developed by John Bowlby, emphasises that children require a secure bond with their primary caregiver, often the mother, to develop a healthy sense of self and the ability to form stable relationships. For mothers, especially those struggling with anxiety related to parenting, attachment-based therapy provides a therapeutic approach that strengthens the emotional bond between parent and child, fostering a foundation of trust, security, and emotional connection.

In attachment-based therapy, mothers are encouraged to explore their own attachment history, often uncovering how their experiences of connection or disconnection in childhood influence their current parenting style and emotional responses. By understanding these patterns, mothers can become more aware of how their behaviors may affect their children's development. For mothers who struggle with anxiety, attachment disruptions—like inconsistent emotional availability, overprotectiveness, or emotional withdrawal—can unintentionally create insecure attachment patterns in their children. Through this therapy, mothers learn to recognise and modify these behaviors, cultivating a more consistent and secure attachment with their child.

The therapeutic process in attachment-based therapy includes practicing attunement, emotional regulation, and responsive caregiving. As mothers develop these skills, they become better equipped to respond calmly and supportively to their children's needs, reducing both their own anxiety and their child's emotional distress. By reinforcing the parent-child bond, attachment-based therapy not only helps anxious mothers build healthier relationships but also enhances children's sense of safety and emotional stability. This therapy supports mothers in developing secure, emotionally resilient family dynamics, promoting long-term well-being for both themselves and their children.

Family Therapy

In 1978, psychiatrist Murray Bowen published Family Therapy in Clinical Practice, a seminal work that consolidated his research and clinical observations, forming the foundation of Bowen Family Systems Theory.

This theory conceptualises the family as an emotional unit, positing that individual behaviors are best understood within the context of family interactions. Bowen introduced key concepts such as differentiation of self, emotional triangles, and the multigenerational transmission process, emphasising how patterns of behavior and emotional functioning are transmitted across generations.

Bowen's approach marked a departure from traditional psychoanalytic methods by focusing on systemic patterns rather than individual pathology. His work has significantly influenced the field of family therapy, providing a framework for understanding and addressing relational dynamics within families. The concepts introduced in his 1978 publication continue to inform therapeutic practices, offering valuable insights into the interconnectedness of family members and the transmission of emotional patterns across generations.

Building upon Bowen's foundational work, family therapy has evolved to recognise the critical role family dynamics play in either perpetuating or alleviating anxiety within the family unit. Anxiety is often not just an individual experience but a shared emotional state influenced by interactions, roles, and patterns established over generations. Family therapy addresses this intergenerational transmission of anxiety by focusing on the emotional and behavioural exchanges that contribute to stress and tension within the family. For mothers and children dealing with anxiety, family therapy provides a supportive space to explore these patterns together, encouraging healthier interactions and emotional resilience.

By involving all family members, family therapy helps each person understand their role in the family's emotional ecosystem. Sessions often highlight how unintentional behaviors, such as overprotection or excessive worry, can reinforce anxiety in others, particularly in children who may absorb these responses. Therapists work collaboratively with the family to recognise these patterns, providing strategies to alter behaviors and establish supportive communication. This approach empowers family members to break cycles of anxious behaviors, fostering understanding, patience, and responsiveness among each other.

The ultimate goal of family therapy is to create a healthier emotional environment where everyone feels heard, understood, and less burdened by unspoken expectations or fears. By learning to express emotions openly and resolve conflicts constructively, family members strengthen their bonds and develop healthier coping mechanisms. This change reduces emotional strain, builds trust, and fosters a resilient family dynamic, helping to protect against the reinforcement of anxiety across generations and promoting long-term emotional well-being for all members.

Hypnotherapy

Hypnotherapy is an effective therapeutic approach for treating anxiety, offering a way to address and transform deep-seated fears and anxieties by accessing the subconscious mind. Through guided relaxation and intense focus, hypnotherapy helps individuals enter a state of heightened awareness, allowing them to bypass conscious barriers and reach core beliefs or memories that may be triggering anxious responses. For parents, especially those dealing with complex, persistent fears or anxieties, this can be invaluable. Hypnotherapy can provide a safe space to explore and process unresolved trauma, such as difficult childbirth experiences or overwhelming fears related to parenting.

During hypnotherapy sessions, individuals can work through these experiences without feeling overwhelmed, often reframing negative beliefs or anxieties that may be reinforcing their symptoms. By addressing these subconscious fears, hypnotherapy can help mothers build a more constructive, calm outlook, breaking patterns of worry that affect their daily lives and interactions with their children. Research has shown that hypnotherapy can lead to long-term relief from anxiety symptoms by helping people reprogram automatic, anxious responses into more balanced, grounded reactions. Additionally, hypnotherapy equips individuals with relaxation techniques that they can use outside of therapy, reinforcing a more peaceful, self-regulated mental state.

Trauma Therapy

Trauma therapy is a powerful approach for treating anxiety, especially when anxiety symptoms stem from past traumatic experiences. Trauma-focused therapy works by helping individuals process and resolve traumatic memories or distressing events that often contribute to chronic anxiety. For individuals with trauma-induced anxiety, therapy can be transformative, as it addresses the root cause of anxiety rather than just managing symptoms. Trauma therapy uses techniques like Eye Movement Desensitisation and Reprocessing (EMDR), Cognitive-Behavioural Therapy (CBT) tailored for trauma, and somatic therapies to help individuals confront, reframe, and integrate traumatic memories.

Through trauma therapy, individuals learn to manage and reduce the intensity of their anxiety responses, which are often heightened by triggers linked to past experiences. By addressing these underlying sources of distress, trauma therapy aims to reduce the "fight-or-flight" responses frequently activated by past trauma. For example, a traumatic event can lead to hypervigilance or a constant state of alertness, both of which are core characteristics of trauma-related anxiety. Therapy helps individuals learn to recognise and cope with these triggers, rewiring their responses so they can engage more fully in the present without constant fear or worry.

This approach to therapy is especially beneficial for those who struggle with trust or safety in relationships, as trauma often disrupts a person's ability to feel secure in their environment. Through careful, supportive exploration of past events, trauma therapy guides individuals in reclaiming a sense of safety, resilience, and control over their emotional responses. It not only alleviates anxiety but also provides tools for managing future stress, enhancing overall mental health and emotional well-being.

Eye Movement Desensitisation and Reprocessing (EMDR)

EMDR (Shapiro, F. 2001) is an innovative therapeutic approach that helps individuals process traumatic or distressing memories. It involves the use of guided eye movements while recalling traumatic events. For mothers who experience anxiety as a result of past trauma, such as a traumatic birth experience, EMDR can be particularly effective in alleviating symptoms. EMDR allows individuals to reprocess distressing events, helping them detach from the emotional weight of those experiences.

Emotional Freedom Technique (EFT)

Also known as "tapping," EFT (Craig, G. 2011) is an accessible, self-administered method that involves tapping on specific acupressure points while focusing on anxiety-inducing thoughts. EFT is rooted in the belief that these actions help to restore balance to the body's energy system. While still emerging as a field of study, EFT has shown promising results in reducing anxiety symptoms, making it a useful complementary tool for anxious mothers.

Medical and Pharmacological Approaches to Anxiety

Medical interventions for anxiety often include pharmacological treatments that regulate neurotransmitter activity in the brain. Commonly prescribed medications target serotonin, norepinephrine, and gamma-aminobutyric acid (GABA) to help manage symptoms such as excessive worry, restlessness, and panic. Selective serotonin reuptake inhibitors (SSRIs) and serotonin-norepinephrine reuptake inhibitors (SNRIs) are frequently used for long-term management, while benzodiazepines may offer short-term relief but require cautious use due to dependency risks. While pharmacological options can be part of an anxiety management plan, they are often integrated with psychotherapy, lifestyle modifications, and stress management techniques for a more comprehensive approach to mental health care.

Seeking Professional Help

Seeking professional help is a crucial step in introducing external support and overcoming barriers to managing anxiety. Medical interventions may be appropriate for identifying and addressing any underlying organic causes of anxiety and for managing severe episodes of dysregulated anxiety. Professional guidance offers tailored, evidence-based strategies that help alleviate anxiety's impact on both parents and their families, fostering a healthier and more supportive environment for emotional well-being.

Conclusion

In conclusion, managing parental anxiety is a continuous journey that involves self-awareness, intentional reflection, and proactive actions. Evolutionary psychology-based therapy approaches provide practical, evidence-based methods to recalibrate anxiety responses. By addressing the root evolutionary mechanisms of anxiety, they offer clients a deeper understanding of their symptoms while equipping them with tools to manage and overcome them effectively. In addition, there are structured approaches such as mindfulness practices, family therapy, or hypnotherapy. By incorporating these therapeutic methods into their lives, parents can work to break the cycle of anxiety, fostering emotional resilience and well-being that supports both their own growth and that of their children. Embracing these strategies opens the path to a healthier, more balanced future for themselves and their families.

Chapter 24:

Critical Stages for Intervention

Addressing parental anxiety at critical stages in life can significantly reduce the likelihood of its transmission to the next generation. Each life stage presents unique challenges and opportunities for intervention, providing a chance to break the cycle of intergenerational anxiety and create healthier environments for children. Below are the key stages where external intervention or deliberate action is most impactful.

Pre-Marriage or Pre-Living Together Arrangements

This stage is foundational, as emotional health patterns and communication dynamics are often established before marriage or cohabitation. Anxiety, if left unaddressed, may set an unhealthy tone for future family life. Interventions during this phase can include resolving childhood or past trauma, couples therapy to foster healthy communication and conflict-resolution skills, stress management and emotional regulation workshops, and education on mental health and its impact on relationships and parenting. These proactive measures help establish a strong emotional foundation for family life.

Pregnancy

Maternal anxiety during pregnancy is particularly critical as it has been linked to increased cortisol levels, which can influence fetal brain development and stress regulation. Interventions during pregnancy include prenatal counselling focused on managing anxiety and building resilience, mindfulness and relaxation techniques such as yoga and meditation, and comprehensive education on the physical and emotional aspects of pregnancy. Partner involvement is also crucial in creating a supportive environment, as shared responsibility can significantly reduce stress for expectant mothers.

The First Three Years of the Child's Life

The first three years of a child's life are a sensitive period for brain development, attachment formation, and emotional regulation. Parental anxiety during this vulnerable time can directly impact a child's sense of security and emotional stability. Support for parents may include joining parenting support groups to normalise challenges and share strategies, accessing early childhood education programs focused on secure attachment and responsive caregiving, and seeking mental health support for postnatal anxiety or depression. Encouraging co-parenting can also help share responsibilities and reduce the overall stress experienced by both parents.

Transition to School (Ages 4–6)

The transition to school marks a child's first exposure to a structured social environment, which can be overwhelming for both children and parents. Parental anxiety during this time may heighten the child's fears and insecurities. Interventions can include workshops for parents on managing separation anxiety, behavioural strategies to support children during transitions, and engaging with school counsellors or child psychologists for additional guidance. These measures ensure children feel supported and secure as they navigate this major life change.

Adolescence

Adolescence brings increased academic, social, and emotional pressures, which can amplify parental anxiety about their child's success or safety. This heightened anxiety can create additional stress within the home. Interventions at this stage may involve family therapy to address communication breakdowns, encouraging autonomy and healthy risk-taking in children, and attending parental workshops on supporting adolescents' mental health and independence. These approaches help parents provide the right balance of guidance and independence.

Divorce

Divorce is a major life event that disrupts family dynamics, creating uncertainty and emotional turmoil for both parents and children. Children are particularly vulnerable during this period as they rely on their caregivers for stability and reassurance. For parents, interventions are required to establish healthy communication and collaborative decision-making, and stress management practices. Building a strong support network of friends, family, or support groups is also vital. For children, interventions could focus on honest but age-appropriate discussions about the divorce to reduce uncertainty, reassurance that the divorce is not their fault, and consistent routines to provide a sense of security. Ensuring access to both parents, where appropriate, can also help reduce feelings of loss or abandonment. Without intervention, parental anxiety during divorce can lead to emotional instability, long-term attachment issues, and perpetuation of intergenerational anxiety.

Major Life Events or Crises

Major life events or crises, such as the death of a family member, chronic illness, financial stress, or relocation, can trigger significant spikes in anxiety. These periods of uncertainty can profoundly influence parenting behaviors and family dynamics. Crisis counselling can help families navigate stress and maintain stability, while support networks provide both emotional and practical assistance. Focused mental health interventions are essential to manage acute anxiety during such times, ensuring that the impact on children is minimised.

Conclusion

Intervening at these critical stages equips parents with the tools to manage anxiety effectively, creating a healthier environment for their children. Each stage offers a unique opportunity for education, therapy, and supportive practices that can prevent the transmission of anxiety to the next generation.

Chapter 25:

Looking Forward: Concluding Comments

As we reach the conclusion of this exploration into parental anxiety and its profound effects on children and future generations, we reflect on the invaluable insights gained throughout this book. The journey has illuminated how parental anxiety influences a child's development from the earliest stages of life, drawing upon scientific theories, clinical observations, and the intricate emotional complexities at play. It is clear that understanding and addressing parental anxiety offers a pathway not just to healing for parents but to creating a legacy of resilience and emotional health for generations to come.

Self-Awareness and Healing

Breaking the cycle of parental anxiety begins with a deep commitment to self-awareness. This publication contributed to raise awareness about the nature of parental anxiety, its transmission, and its impact. Parents who recognise their anxiety triggers, understand how these emotions influence their behaviors, and acknowledge the impact on their children take a crucial first step toward healing. This level of insight empowers intentional change, helping parents develop healthier ways to respond to stress and guide their children through difficult emotions.

Seeking help as a parent is an act of courage and strength, particularly for mothers, whose emotional well-being profoundly shapes their children's development. Addressing parental anxiety is not merely about reducing stress; it is about cultivating emotional resilience that benefits both parent and child. When parents learn to navigate their anxiety effectively, they foster emotional stability in their homes and model adaptive coping mechanisms for their children. This ripple effect creates a foundation of emotional health and resilience that can influence not just their children but future generations.

Focusing on What Can Be Controlled

For parents experiencing anxiety, focusing on aspects of life within their control is a starting point of an effective strategy to manage overwhelming feelings. While it is impossible to control every element of a child's life, parents can ensure a stable and supportive environment by prioritising essentials like proper nutrition, consistent sleep, physical activity, and a predictable routine. Taking action in these areas reduces the emotional burden of anxiety and fosters a healthier home atmosphere. Recognising when challenges feel insurmountable and seeking external support, whether through therapy, community resources, or medical professionals, is an essential step toward addressing complex issues.

The principle that "quality of life is never an accident" underscores this approach. A meaningful and fulfilling life requires conscious decisions, beginning with self-reflection and recognition of the factors impacting mental and physical well-being. Self-awareness opens the door to change, and seeking therapeutic help provides the tools and support needed to navigate emotional challenges. In this way, the journey toward improved mental health and quality of life for both parents and children starts with the courage to ask for help.

A Positive Outlook on Anxiety Treatment

This book does not present a grim narrative of anxiety's impact but instead offers a hopeful perspective on recovery. Modern treatment models, especially those informed by evolutionary psychology, provide effective methods to recalibrate the overactive alarm systems underlying anxiety. Viewing anxiety as an adaptive mechanism that has become maladaptive in certain contexts helps normalise the experience and reduce stigma.

For less complex anxiety disorders like generalised anxiety disorder (GAD) or specific phobias, evidence-based approaches such as Cognitive Behavioural Therapy (CBT) and Mindfulness-Based Stress Reduction (MBSR) often yield significant improvement within a matter of months. In contrast, more complex cases involving trauma, comorbid conditions, or chronic patterns may require multimodal, trauma-informed therapies that demand longer-term commitment but deliver meaningful progress. Regardless of the complexity, modern treatments offer a pathway to healing, highlighting that anxiety, even when severe, is treatable with the right approach.

Critical Stages for Intervention

Prevention is the most powerful tool in addressing parental anxiety. Early interventions at critical life stages can significantly reduce the likelihood of anxiety transmission to the next generation. This book highlights key stages for intervention, including pre-marriage, pregnancy, the first three years of a child's life, the transition to school age, adolescence, divorce, and major family life events or crises. Each stage presents unique challenges and opportunities to implement targeted strategies that equip parents to manage anxiety effectively and create healthier environments for their children.

While this publication does not propose specific policy solutions, it emphasises the importance of addressing parental anxiety at these pivotal stages. Intervening through education, therapy, and supportive practices at these critical stages ensures better outcomes for both parents and children. These interventions foster emotional stability and resilience, laying the foundation for a more emotionally secure future and breaking the cycle of intergenerational anxiety.

Long-Term Resilience for Children

Breaking the cycle of parental anxiety is essential for fostering emotional resilience in children. Anxiety evolved as an adaptive mechanism to protect against threats, but when excessively heightened or misdirected in parents, it can inadvertently signal to children that the world is consistently dangerous. By learning to regulate their own anxiety, parents model balanced responses to stress, providing children with a healthier blueprint for managing their emotions.

This adaptive modelling equips children with critical skills such as emotional regulation, problem-solving, and self-awareness. These tools enable them to confidently navigate life's challenges, from social pressures to academic demands. In evolutionary terms, children who observe and learn from calm, emotionally stable caregivers develop internal mechanisms to assess and respond to threats more appropriately. Teaching children to set realistic goals, openly discuss emotions, and value effort over outcomes reinforces their ability to adapt and thrive in complex environments, laying the groundwork for lifelong mental wellness.

The Ripple Effect of Breaking the Cycle

Addressing parental anxiety has far-reaching effects that extend beyond the immediate parent-child relationship, shaping family dynamics, strengthening communities, and influencing future generations. From an evolutionary psychology perspective, parents play a critical role in modelling emotional resilience, a fundamental trait for a child's development. Children raised by emotionally stable parents are better equipped to form strong social bonds, empathise with others, and contribute positively to their communities—traits vital for survival and cooperation in both ancestral and modern contexts.

This ripple effect also drives broader societal change. By fostering emotional resilience and addressing anxiety, parents contribute to a culture that values mental health and reduces the stigma of seeking help. Resilient individuals enhance their communities by building supportive networks and fostering empathy. Children raised in emotionally secure households are more likely to pursue fulfilling careers, maintain healthy relationships, and actively engage in society. Breaking the cycle of parental anxiety benefits not only individual families but also lays the groundwork for a healthier, more adaptable, and resilient society prepared to navigate contemporary challenges.

Shaping Future Generations

Breaking the cycle of parental anxiety has the profound potential to transform family lineages and influence future generations. Children raised in emotionally stable environments with secure attachments are more likely to develop resilience, emotional intelligence, and healthy coping mechanisms. These traits, in turn, are passed on to their children, creating a generational legacy of emotional well-being and stability.

Parents who actively work to manage their anxiety are not just improving their own lives but reshaping the future for their children and grandchildren. By modelling emotional regulation, fostering open communication, and creating a nurturing environment, they lay a foundation where anxiety is managed constructively, and resilience becomes the norm. This legacy extends outward to strengthen communities, contributing to a society that prioritises emotional wellness and perpetuates resilience across generations.

A Hopeful Path Forward

This book has illuminated the critical aspects of parental anxiety, its transmission, and its impact across generations. Breaking the cycle of anxiety is undoubtedly challenging, but it is deeply rewarding. Awareness of the profound effects of parental anxiety is the first step. When understood and addressed, parental anxiety becomes an opportunity to cultivate emotional resilience and foster healthier family dynamics.

The hopeful message of this book is that the cycle of anxiety can indeed be broken. Every step a parent takes toward understanding, taking deliberate action, and managing their anxiety creates a ripple effect, leaving a lasting impact on their own life and on future generations. By prioritising mental health, taking deliberate action, modelling adaptive coping strategies, and fostering secure emotional connections, parents have the power to establish a legacy of strength, stability, and well-being. This legacy lays the foundation for a brighter future where families are more connected, resilient, and prepared to navigate the complexities of modern life with confidence and compassion.

Appendices

References

Abramowitz, J. S. (2006). The psychological treatment of obsessive-compulsive disorder. The Canadian Journal of Psychiatry, 51(7), 407–416. DOI: 10.1177/070674370605100703

Abramowitz, J. S. (2006). Understanding and Treating Obsessive-Compulsive Disorder: A Cognitive Behavioural Approach. Lawrence Erlbaum Associates.

Ainsworth, M. D. S., Blehar, M. C., Waters, E., & Wall, S. (1978). Patterns of Attachment: A Psychological Study of the Strange Situation. Lawrence Erlbaum Associates

Aldao, A., Nolen-Hoeksema, S., & Schweizer, S. (2010). Emotion-regulation strategies across psychopathology: A meta-analytic review. Clinical Psychology Review, 30(2), 217–237.

Amato, P. R. (2000). The consequences of divorce for adults and children. Journal of Marriage and Family, 62(4), 1269–1287. DOI: 10.1111/j.1741-3737.2000.01269.x

American Psychological Association (APA): https://www.apa.org/topics/anxiety

Andrea L. Hinds a, Erik Z. Woody b, Ana Drandic a, Louis A. Schmidt c, Michael Van Ameringena, Marie Coroneos a, Henry Szechtmana, (2010) The psychology of potential threat: Properties of the security motivation system. Biological Psychology Journal.

Asmundson, G. J. G., & Taylor, S. (2005). It's not all in your head: How worrying about your health could be making you sick—and what you can do about it. Guilford Press.

Australian Institute of Health and Welfare (2024). Perinatal mental health screening in Australia.

Australian Bureau of Statistics (2020–2022), National Study of Mental Health and Wellbeing.

Balshine, S. (2012). Patterns of parental care in vertebrates. Encyclopedia of Life Sciences.

Bandura, A. (1963). Social Learning and Personality Development. New York, NY: Holt, Rinehart, and Winston.

Bandura, A. (1977). Social Learning Theory. Englewood Cliffs, NJ: Prentice-Hall.

Bandura, A. (1986). Social Foundations of Thought and Action: A Social Cognitive Theory. Englewood Cliffs, NJ: Prentice-Hall.

Bandura, A. (2001). Social cognitive theory: An agentic perspective. Annual Review of Psychology, 52, 1–26. DOI: 10.1146/annurev.psych.52.1.1

Bandura, A., Ross, D., & Ross, S. A. (1961). Transmission of aggression through imitation of aggressive models. Journal of Abnormal and Social Psychology, 63(3), 575–582.

Barlow, D. H. (2002). Anxiety and Its Disorders: The Nature and Treatment of Anxiety and Panic (2nd ed.). Guilford Press.

Barrett, P. M., & Turner, C. M. (2001). "Prevention of anxiety symptoms in primary school children: Preliminary results from a universal school-based trial." The British Journal of Clinical Psychology, 40(4), 399-410.

Baumrind, D. (1967). Child care practices anteceding three patterns of preschool behavior. Genetic Psychology Monographs, 75(1), 43–88.

Beck, A. T., & Clark, D. A. (1997). "An information processing model of anxiety: Automatic and strategic processes." Behaviour Research and Therapy, 35(1), 49-58.

Beck, C. T. (2001). Predictors of postpartum depression: An update. Nursing Research, 50(5), 275–285. DOI: 10.1097/00006199-200109000-00004

Bentley, M. E., Gavin, L., Black, M. M., & Teti, L. O. (1999). Infant feeding practices and maternal role decisions in the first year of life. Journal of Nutrition Education.

Biaggi, A., Conroy, S., Pawlby, S., & Pariante, C. M. (2016). Identifying the women at risk of antenatal anxiety and depression: A systematic review. Journal of Affective Disorders, 191, 62–77. DOI: 10.1016/j.jad.2015.11.014

Bjorklund, D. F., & Pellegrini, A. D. (2000). Child Development and Evolutionary Psychology. Child Development, 71(6), 1687–1708. DOI: 10.1111/1467-8624.00258

Bjorklund, D. F., & Pellegrini, A. D. (2002). The Origins of Human Nature: Evolutionary Developmental Psychology. American Psychological Association. DOI: 10.1037/10425-000

Bögels, S. M., & Brechman-Toussaint, M. L. (2006). Family Issues in Child Anxiety: Attachment, Family Functioning, Parental Rearing and Beliefs. Clinical Psychology Review, 26(7), 834–856.

Bögels, S. M., & Phares, V. (2008). "Parents' Role in the Etiology of Child Anxiety: A Review and Model for Future Research." Clinical Psychology Review, 28(4), 539–558.

Bonomi, A. E., Anderson, M. L., Rivara, F. P., & Thompson, R. S. (2007). Health outcomes in women with physical and sexual intimate partner violence exposure. Journal of Women's Health, 16(7), 987–997.

Bos, H. M. W., van Balen, F., & van den Boom, D. C. (2007). Child adjustment and parenting in planned lesbian-parent families. American Journal of Orthopsychiatry, 77(1), 38–48. DOI: 10.1037/0002-9432.77.1.38

Bowen, M. (1978). Family Therapy in Clinical Practice. Jason Aronson, Inc.

Bowlby, J. (1969). Attachment and loss: Vol. 1. Attachment. New York: Basic Books.

Bowlby, J. (1980). Attachment and Loss: Volume 3. Loss, Sadness and Depression. Basic Books.

Bowlby, J. (1988). A Secure Base: Parent-Child Attachment and Healthy Human Development.

Bronfenbrenner, U. (1979). The Ecology of Human Development: Experiments by Nature and Design. Harvard University Press.

Brown, B. (2012). Daring Greatly: How the Courage to Be Vulnerable Transforms the Way We Live, Love, Parent, and Lead. Gotham Books.

Brown, J. L., Morales, V., & Summers, K. (2010). Divergence in parental care, habitat selection, and larval life history among four species of peruvian poison frogs. Journal of Evolutionary Biology, 23(8), 1735–1747.

Buglio, Gabriele Lo., Erika Cerasti, Tommaso Boldrini, Ciro Conversano, Vittorio Lingiardi Lingiardi, Annalisa Tanzilli (2024). Defense mechanisms in individuals with depressive and anxiety symptoms: a network analysis. Fronteers in Psychology. Vol 15. https://doi.org/10.3389/fpsyg.2024.1465164

Bullmore, Edward. (2019). The Inflamed Mind – A Radical New Approach to Depression. Printed at CPI Group UK Ltd. Crydon

Buss, D. M. (1989). Sex differences in human mate preferences: Evolutionary hypotheses tested in 37 cultures. *Behavioral and Brain Sciences, 12*(1), 1-49.

Carbone-López, K., Kruttschnitt, C., & Macmillan, R. (2006). Patterns of intimate partner violence and their associations with physical health, psychological distress, and substance use. Public Health Reports, 121(4), 382–392.

Carter, C. S. (1998). Neuroendocrine perspectives on social attachment and love. Psychoneuroendocrinology, 23(8), 779–818.

Chabert, T., et al. (2015). Parental care in reptiles. Behavioral Ecology and Sociobiology, 69(6), 891–898.

Clark, D. M., & Wells, A. (1995). A cognitive model of social phobia. In R. G. Heimberg, M. R. Liebowitz, D. A. Hope, & F. R. Schneier (Eds.), Social Phobia: Diagnosis, Assessment, and Treatment (pp. 69–93). Guilford Press.

Coker, A. L., Davis, K. E., Arias, I., Desai, S., Sanderson, M., Brandt, H. M., & Smith, P. H. (2002). Physical and mental health effects of intimate partner violence for men and women. American Journal of Preventive Medicine, 23(4), 260–268.

Coltrane, S. (2000). Research on household labor: Modeling and measuring the social embeddedness of routine family work. Journal of Marriage and Family, 62(4), 1208–1233.

Compas, B. E., Connor-Smith, J. K., Saltzman, H., Thomsen, A. H., & Wadsworth, M. E. (2001). "Coping with Stress during Childhood and Adolescence: Problems, Progress, and Potential in Theory and Research." Psychological Bulletin, 127(1), 87–127.

Compas, B. E., Ey, S., & Grant, K. E. (1993). Taxonomy, assessment, and diagnosis of depression during adolescence. Psychological Bulletin, 114(2), 323–344. DOI: 10.1037/0033-2909.114.2.323

Craig, G. (2011). The EFT Manual (2nd Edition). Energy Psychology Press. ISBN: 978-1604150667

Craske, M. G., & Barlow, D. H. (2007). Mastery of Your Anxiety and Panic: Workbook for Primary Care Settings (4th ed.). Oxford University Press. DOI: 10.1093/med:psych/ 9780195311402.001.0001

Daniel Nettle (2004). Evolutionary origins of depression: a review and reformulation. In Journal of Affective Disorders 81 (2004) 91 – 102

Danquah, Adam N. and Katherine Berry (2014). Attachment Theory in Adult Mental Health. A guide to clinical practice. Edited by. Routledge

Daws, Dilys and de Rementeria, Alexandra (2022). Finding Your Way With Youe Baby - The Emotional Life of Parents and Babies. Second edition

Debra Kissen, Micah Ioffe, Hannah Romain, (2022). Overcoming parental anxiety : rewire your brain to worry less and enjoy parenting more. Oakland, CA : New Harbinger Publications, [2022]

Dennis C, Falah-Hassani K and Shiri R (2017) 'Prevalence of antenatal and postnatal anxiety: Systematic review and meta-analysis- external site opens in new window', The British Journal of Psychiatry, 210(5), 315–323, doi:10.1192/bjp.bp.116.187179.

Dennis, C. L., Hodnett, E., Kenton, L., Weston, J., Zupancic, J., Stewart, D. E., & Kiss, A. (2009). Effect of peer support on prevention of postnatal depression among high-risk women:

Multisite randomised controlled trial. BMJ, 338, a3064. DOI: 10.1136/bmj.a3064

Dube, S. R., Anda, R. F., Felitti, V. J., Edwards, V. J., & Croft, J. B. (2002). Adverse childhood experiences and personal alcohol abuse as an adult. Addictive Behaviors, 27(5), 713–725.

Dugas, M. J., & Ladouceur, R. (2000). "Treatment of GAD: Targeting intolerance of uncertainty in two types of worry." Behavior Modification, 24(5), 635-657.

Dunkel Schetter, C. (2011). Psychological science on pregnancy: Stress processes, biopsychosocial models, and emerging research issues. Annual Review of Psychology, 62, 531–558. DOI: 10.1146/annurev.psych.031809.130727

Eccles, J. S., & Roeser, R. W. (2011). "Schools as Developmental Contexts during Adolescence." Journal of Research on Adolescence, 21(1), 225–241.

Ein-Dor, T., Mikulincer, M., Doron, G., & Shaver, P. R. (2010). The attachment paradox: How can so many of us (the insecure ones) have no adaptive advantages? Perspectives on Psychological Science, 5(2), 123–141.

Eisenberg, N., & Strayer, J. (Eds.). (1987). Empathy and Its Development. Cambridge University Press.

Erikson, E. H. (1968). Identity: Youth and Crisis. Norton & Company.

Evans, G. W., Li, D., & Whipple, S. S. (2008). Cumulative risk and child development. Psychological Bulletin, 134(6), 920–940. DOI: 10.1037/a0013340

Felitti, V. J., Anda, R. F., Nordenberg, D., Williamson, D. F., Spitz, A. M., Edwards, V., ... & Marks, J. S. (1998). Relationship of childhood abuse and household dysfunction to many of the leading causes of death in adults: The Adverse Childhood Experiences (ACE) Study. American Journal of Preventive Medicine, 14(4), 245–258.

Field, A. P., & Lester, K. J. (2010). Is there room for "development" in developmental models of information processing biases to threat in children and adolescents? Clinical Child and Family

Psychology Review, 13(4), 315–332. DOI: 10.1007/s10567-010-0078-8

Fincham, F. D., & Beach, S. R. H. (2010). Marriage in the new millennium: A decade in review. Journal of Marriage and Family, 72(3), 630–649.

Flett, G. L., Hewitt, P. L., & Singer, A. (2002). "Perfectionism and Parental Authority Styles: An Interactive Model of Trait Perfectionism and Family Processes." Journal of Personality and Social Psychology, 82(3), 431–440.

Fraley, R. C., & Shaver, P. R. (2000). Adult romantic attachment: Theoretical developments, emerging controversies, and unanswered questions. Review of General Psychology, 4(2), 132–154.

Freud, S. (1937). The Ego and the Mechanisms of Defence.

Gelso, C. J., & Hayes, J. A. (2007). Countertransference and the Therapist's Inner Experience.

Giedd, J. N., & Rapoport, J. L. (2010). Structural MRI of paediatric brain development: What have we learned and where are we going? Neuron, 67(5), 728–734. DOI: 10.1016/j.neuron.2010.08.040

Glover, V. (2011). Annual Research Review: Prenatal stress and the origins of psychopathology: An evolutionary perspective. Journal of Child Psychology and Psychiatry, 52(4), 356–367. DOI: 10.1111/j.1469-7610.2011.02371.x

Glover, V. (2014). Maternal Anxiety During Pregnancy and Its Effects on the Fetus and Child. In Perinatal Programming of Neurodevelopment (pp. 9-22). Springer.

Glover, V. (2014). Maternal depression, anxiety and stress during pregnancy and child outcome; What needs to be done. Best Practice & Research: Clinical Obstetrics & Gynaecology, 28(1), 25–35. DOI: 10.1016/j.bpobgyn.2013.08.017

Glover, V., O'Connor, T. G., & O'Donnell, K. (2010). Prenatal stress and the programming of the HPA axis. Neuroscience and Biobehavioral Reviews, 35(1), 17–22. DOI: 10.1016/j.neubiorev.2009.11.008

Goodwin, N. B., et al. (1998). Evolutionary transitions in parental care in fishes. Proceedings of the Royal Society of London. Series B: Biological Sciences, 265(1405), 2265–2272.

Green, Viviane (ed) (2003). Emotional Development in Psychoanalysis, Attachment Theory and Neuroscience. Routledge

Gregory, A. M., & Eley, T. C. (2007). Genetic influences on anxiety in children: What we've learned and where we're heading. Clinical Child and Family Psychology Review, 10(3), 199–212. DOI: 10.1007/s10567-007-0022-8

Groenewald, C. B., Essner, B. S., Wright, D., Fesinmeyer, M. D., & Palermo, T. M. (2014). "The economic costs of chronic pain among a cohort of treatment-seeking adolescents in the United States." The Journal of Pain, 15(9), 925-933.

Gunnar, M. R. (2007). Stress and Emotion in Early Development. Handbook of Developmental Cognitive Neuroscience (2nd ed.), 106-113. MIT Press.

Hayes, S. C., Strosahl, K. D., & Wilson, K. G. (2012). Acceptance and Commitment Therapy: The Process and Practice of Mindful Change (2nd Edition). The Guilford Press. ISBN: 978-1609189624

Hays, S. (1996). The cultural contradictions of motherhood. Yale University Press.

Heidi Keller (2018). Universality claim of attachment theory: Children's socioemotional development across cultures. Proceedings of the National Academy of Sciences, 115(45), 11414–11419.

Helen Dent. (2019). Why Don't I Feel Good Enough? Using Attachment Theory to Find a Solution. Routledge

Herrenkohl, T. I., Hong, S., Klika, J. B., Herrenkohl, R. C., & Russo, M. J. (2008). Developmental impacts of child abuse and exposure to domestic violence. Trauma, Violence, & Abuse, 9(2), 84–99. DOI: 10.1177/1524838008314797

Hettema, J. M., Neale, M. C., & Kendler, K. S. (2001). A review and meta-analysis of the genetic epidemiology of anxiety disorders. American Journal of Psychiatry, 158(10), 1568–1578. DOI: 10.1176/appi.ajp.158.10.1568

Hrdy, S. B. (1999). *Mother Nature: Maternal Instincts and How They Shape the Human Species*. Ballantine Books.

Javaid, S.F., Hashim, I.J., Hashim, M.J. et al. (2023). Epidemiology of anxiety disorders: global burden and sociodemographic associations. Middle East Curr Psychiatry 30, 44 (2023). https://doi.org/10.1186/s43045-023-00315-3

Journal of the American Academy of Child & Adolescent Psychiatry, 42(3), 290–297. DOI: 10.1097/00004583-200303000-00012

Judy L. Silberg,1 Hermine Maes,1 and Lindon J. Eaves (2011). Genetic and environmental influences on the transmission of parental depression to children's depression and conduct disturbance: An extended Children of Twins study. J Child Psychol Psychiatry. doi: 10.1111/j.1469-7610.2010.02205.x

Kagan, J. (1984). The nature of the child. New York, NY: Basic Books.

Kagan, J., Reznick, J. S., & Snidman, N. (1988). Biological bases of childhood shyness. Science, 240(4849), 167–171. DOI: 10.1126/science.3353713

Kagitcibasi, C. (2007). Family, Self, and Human Development Across Cultures: Theory and Applications. Lawrence Erlbaum Associates.

Kahn, M. (1997). Between Therapist and Client: The New Relationship.

Kamalpreet Rakhra, (2017). Maternal Depression and Anxiety and impact on physical, Cognitive and Emotional Development of Children at Three Years of Age. PhD Thesis, University of Saskatchewan,

Karl Heinz Brisch. (2011). Treating Attachment Disorders: From Theory to Therapy. THE GUILFORD PRESS.

Kasalova et al. (2020). Marriage in panic: Panic disorder and intimate relationships. Neuroendocrinology Letters, 41(4), 181-190. Available online: www.nel.edu .

Kessler, R. C., Berglund, P., Demler, O., Jin, R., Merikangas, K. R., & Walters, E. E. (2005). Lifetime prevalence and age-of-onset distributions of DSM-IV disorders in the National Comorbidity Survey Replication. Archives of General Psychiatry, 62(6), 593–602. DOI: 10.1001/archpsyc.62.6.593

Kessler, R. C., Chiu, W. T., Demler, O., & Walters, E. E. (2005). Prevalence, Severity, and Comorbidity of 12-month DSM-IV Disorders in the National Comorbidity Survey Replication (NCS-R). Archives of General Psychiatry, 62(6), 617-627.

Kissen, D., Ioffe, M., & Romain, H. (2022). Overcoming Parental Anxiety: Rewire Your Brain to Worry Less and Raise Calm, Resilient Kids. New Harbinger Publications. ISBN: 978-1684039256

Kitzmann, K. M., Gaylord, N. K., Holt, A. R., & Kenny, E. D. (2003). Child witnesses to domestic violence: A meta-analytic review. Journal of Consulting and Clinical Psychology, 71(2), 339–352. DOI: 10.1037/0022-006X.71.2.339

Kleiman, D. G. (1977). Monogamy in mammals. Quarterly Review of Biology, 52(1), 39–69.

Konner, M. (2010). The Evolution of Childhood: Relationships, Emotion, Mind.

Laith Al-Shawaf1,2 and David M. G. Lewis. (2017) Evolutionary Psychology and the Emotions. In V. Zeigler-Hill, T.K. Shackelford (eds.), Encyclopedia of Personality and Individual Differences, # Springer International Publishing AG 2017. DOI 10.1007/978-3-319-28099-8_516-1

Lamb, M. E. (Ed.). (2010). The Role of the Father in Child Development (5th ed.). Hoboken, NJ: John Wiley & Sons.

Lamb, M. E., Thompson, R. A., Gardner, W. P., Charnov, E. L., & Estes, D. (1985). Infant-mother attachment: The origins and developmental significance of individual differences in Strange Situation behavior. Behavioral and Brain Sciences, 8(1), 129–171.

Lareau, A. (2003). Unequal Childhoods: Class, Race, and Family Life. University of California Press.

Leahy-Warren, P., McCarthy, G., & Corcoran, P. (2012). First-Time Mothers: Social Support, Maternal Parental Self-Efficacy and Postnatal Depression. Journal of Clinical Nursing, 21(3-4), 388-397.

Leahy-Warren, P., McCarthy, G., & Corcoran, P. (2012). Postnatal depression in first-time mothers. Archives of Psychiatric Nursing, 26(1), 44–53. DOI: 10.1016/j.apnu.2011.03.005

LeDoux, J. E. (2000). Emotion circuits in the brain. Annual Review of Neuroscience, 23, 155–184. DOI: 10.1146/annurev.neuro.23.1.155

Levine, S. (2005). Developmental Determinants of Sensitivity and Resistance to Stress. Psycho-neuroendocrinology, 30(10), 939-946.

Lewis, M., Feiring, C., & Rosenthal, S. (2000). Attachment over time. Child Development, 71(3), 707–720.

Lipton, B. H. (2005). The Biology of Belief: Unleashing the Power of Consciousness, Matter, and Miracles. Mountain of Love/Elite Books

Lukas, D., & Clutton-Brock, T. H. (2013). The evolution of social monogamy in mammals. Science, 341(6145), 526–530.

Luthar, S. S., & Barkin, S. H. (2012). Are affluent youth truly "at risk"? Vulnerability and resilience across three diverse samples. Development and Psychopathology, 24(2), 429–449.

Luthar, S. S., & Latendresse, S. J. (2005). Children of the affluent: Challenges to well-being. Current Directions in Psychological Science, 14(1), 49–53. DOI: 10.1111/j.0963-7214.2005.00333.x

Lythcott-Haims, J. (2015). How to Raise an Adult: Break Free of the Overparenting Trap and Prepare Your Kid for Success. Henry Holt and Company. ISBN: 978-1627791779

Man Him Ho, Benjamin Thomas Kemp, Hedwig Eisenbarth, Ronald J.P. Rijnders (2023). Designing a neuro-clinical assessment of empathy deficits in psychopathy based on the Zipper Model of Empathy. Neuroscience & Biobehavioral Reviews Volume 151, August 2023, 105244

Margolin, G., & Vickerman, K. A. (2007). Posttraumatic stress in children and adolescents exposed to family violence: I. Overview and issues. Professional Psychology: Research and Practice, 38(6), 613–619. DOI: 10.1037/0735-7028.38.6.613

Marks, I. M. (2001). Living with Fear: Understanding and Coping with Anxiety.

Marks, I. M., & Nesse, R. M. (1994). Fear and fitness: An evolutionary analysis of anxiety disorders. Ethology and Sociobiology, 15(5-6), 247–261.

Masten, A. S. (2001). "Ordinary Magic: Resilience Processes in Development." American Psychologist, 56(3), 227–238.

Masten, A. S., & Reed, M.-G. J. (2005). Resilience in development. In C. R. Snyder & S. J. Lopez (Eds.), Handbook of Positive Psychology (pp. 74–88). Oxford University Press.

Matthey, S., Barnett, B., Howie, P., & Kavanagh, D. J. (2003). Diagnosing postpartum depression in mothers and fathers: Whatever happened to anxiety? Journal of Affective Disorders, 74(2), 139–147. DOI: 10.1016/S0165-0327(02)00012-5

McConnell, Megan (2008). "Attachment, depression, and perceptions of parenting among adolescent mothers" Master's Theses. 3537. DOI: https://doi.org/10.31979/etd.ub74-xr4t

Meaney, M. J. (2001). Maternal care, gene expression, and the transmission of individual differences in stress reactivity across generations. *Annual Review of Neuroscience, 24*(1), 1161–1192.

Mineka, S., & Cook, M. (1988). Social learning and the acquisition of snake fear in monkeys. Advances in Behaviour Research and Therapy, 10(4), 211–236. DOI: 10.1016/0146 6402(88)90013-8

Minuchin, S. (1974). Families and Family Therapy. Harvard University Press.

Montgomery, N. (2010). Helicopter parenting and its effect on college students' well-being. Presented at the 2010 Meeting of the Society for Personality and Social Psychology.

Morris, A. S., Silk, J. S., Steinberg, L., Myers, S. S., & Robinson, L. R. (2007). "The role of the family context in the development of emotion regulation." Social Development, 16(2), 361-388.

Mulder, C. H., & Wagner, M. (1998). First-time homeownership in the family life course: A West German-Dutch comparison. Urban Studies.

Murray, L., Cooper, P., Creswell, C., Schofield, E., & Sack, C. (2009). "The Effects of Maternal Social Phobia on Mother–Infant Interactions and Infant Social Responsiveness." Journal of Child Psychology and Psychiatry, 48(1), 45–52.

Murray, L., Creswell, C., & Cooper, P. J. (2009). "The development of anxiety disorders in childhood: An integrative review." Psychological Medicine, 39(9), 1413-1423.

Music, Graham. (2017) Nurturing Natures: Attachment and Children's Emotional, Sociocultural and Brain Development. Second Edition. Routledge.

National Institute of Mental Health (NIMH): https://www.nimh.nih.gov/health/topics/anxiety-disorders

Nesse R M (2022). Anxiety Disorders in Evolutionary Perspective. In RT Abed & PS John Smith (Eds). Evolutionary Psychiatry: Current Perspectives in Evolution and Mental Health. Cambridge University Press.

Nesse, R. M. (1994). Fear and fitness: An evolutionary analysis of anxiety disorders. Ethology and Sociobiology, 15(5-6), 247–261.

Nesse, R. M. (2000). Is depression an adaptation? Archives of General Psychiatry, 57(1), 14–20.

Nesse, R. M., & Williams, G. C. (1994). Why We Get Sick: The New Science of Darwinian Medicine.

Neumann, Inga D., Alexa H. Veenema, and Daniela I. Beiderbeck (2010) Aggression and anxiety: social context and neurobiological links. Frontiers in Behavioral Neuroscience. Volume 4 - 2010 | https://doi.org/10.3389/fnbeh.2010.00012

Numan, M., & Insel, T. R. (2003). The Neurobiology of Parental Behavior. Springer.

Numan, M., & Young, L. J. (2015). Neural mechanisms of mother-infant bonding and pair bonding: Similarities, differences, and broader implications. doi:10.1016/j.yhbeh.2015.05.015

Numan, M., & Young, L. J. (2016). Neural mechanisms of maternal behavior in mammals. Encyclopedia of Animal Behavior.

Numan, Michael (2020) The Parental Brain: Mechanisms, Development, and Evolution. Oxford.

Odent, M. (2001). The Caesarean. Free Association Books.

O'Donnell, K., O'Connor, T. G., & Glover, V. (2009). Prenatal stress and neurodevelopment of the child: Focus on the HPA axis and role of the placenta. Developmental Neuroscience, 31(4), 285–292.

Paquette, D. (2004). Theorizing the father-child relationship: Mechanisms and developmental outcomes. Human Development, 47(4), 193–219.

Philippa Perry (2019). The Book You Wish Your Parents Had Read. Penguins Random House.

Pine, D. S., & Fox, N. A. (2015). Childhood antecedents and risk for adult mental disorders. Annual Review of Psychology, 66, 459–485. DOI: 10.1146/annurev-psych-010814-015038

Pluess, M., & Belsky, J. (2010). Differential susceptibility to rearing experience: The case of childcare. Journal of Child Psychology and Psychiatry, 51(4), 428–434.

Porges, S. W. (2011). The Polyvagal Theory: Neurophysiological Foundations of Emotions, Attachment, Communication, and Self-Regulation. W. W. Norton & Company. ISBN: 978-0393707007

Prior, Vivien and Glaser, Danya (2006). Understanding Attachment and Attachment Disorders: Theory, Evidence and Practice. Jessica Kingsley Publishers

Puckering, Christine. (1987) The Impact of Maternal Depression on Young Children. Article in Journal of Child Psychology and Psychiatry · December 1987. DOI: 10.1111/j.1752-0118.1988.tb01026.x · Source: PubMed

Raley, S., Mattingly, M., & Bianchi, S. (2006). How dual are dual-income couples? Documenting change from 1970 to 2001. Journal of Marriage and Family.

Rapee, R. M., Schniering, C. A., & Hudson, J. L. (2009). "Anxiety disorders during childhood and adolescence: Origins and treatment." Annual Review of Clinical Psychology, 5, 311-341.

Rich, Phil. (2006). Attachment and Sexual Offending Understanding and Applying Attachment Theory to the Treatment of Juvenile Sexual Offenders. John Wiley.

Rutter, M. (1981). Maternal deprivation reassessed. London: Penguin.

Rutter, M. (1995). Clinical implications of attachment concepts: Retrospect and prospect. Journal of Child Psychology and Psychiatry, 36(4), 549–571.

Ryan, R. M., & Deci, E. L. (2000). Self-determination theory and the facilitation of intrinsic motivation, social development, and well-being. American Psychologist, 55(1), 68–78. DOI: 10.1037/0003-066X.55.1.68

Salkovskis, P. M. (1985). Obsessional-compulsive problems: A cognitive-behavioural analysis. Behaviour Research and Therapy, 23(5), 571–583. DOI: 10.1016/0005-7967(85)90105-6

Schaffer, H. R., & Emerson, P. E. (1964). The development of social attachments in infancy. Monographs of the Society for Research in Child Development, 29(3), 1–77.

Schneider, B., Hastings, N., & Laureau, A. (2006). The ambitious generation: America's teenagers, motivated but directionless.

Seligman, M. E. P. (1972). Learned helplessness. Annual Review of Medicine, 23(1), 407–412. DOI: 10.1146/annurev.me.23.020172.002203

Shapiro, F. (2001). Eye Movement Desensitization and Reprocessing: Basic Principles, Protocols, and Procedures (2nd Edition). The Guilford Press. ISBN: 978-1572306721

Shonkoff, J. P., & Phillips, D. A. (Eds.). (2000). From Neurons to Neighborhoods: The Science of Early Childhood Development. National Academy Press. DOI: 10.17226/9824

Slade, Pauline. Et al (2020) Do stress and anxiety in early pregnancy affect the progress of labor: Evidence from the Wirral Child Health and Development Study. DOI: 10.1111/aogs.14063.

Smoller, J. W., Andreassen, O. A., Edenberg, H. J., Faraone, S. V., Glatt, S. J., & Kendler, K. S. (2009). Genetic associations with psychiatric disorders: The emerging role of the integrative genomics approach. World Psychiatry, 8(3), 159–168. DOI: 10.1002/j.2051-5545.2009.tb00250

Stein, M. B., & Smoller, J. W. (2018). The genetics of anxiety disorders: What's new? Biological Psychiatry, 83(10), 894–904. DOI: 10.1016/j.biopsych.2017.10.007.

Stein, M. B., Jang, K. L., Taylor, S., Vernon, P. A., & Livesley, W. J. (2018). Genetic and environmental influences on trauma exposure and posttraumatic stress disorder symptoms: A twin study. American Journal of Psychiatry, 175(7), 654–662.

Steinberg, L. (2001). We Know Some Things: Parent-Adolescent Relationships in Retrospect and Prospect. Cambridge University Press.

Stuart, S., & O'Hara, M. W. (1995). Interpersonal psychotherapy for postpartum depression: A treatment program. Journal of Psychotherapy Practice and Research, 4(1), 18–29.

Stuart, S., & O'Hara, M. W. (1995). Postpartum Depression: The Influence of Health and Personality Factors. Journal of Psychosomatic Research, 39(1), 51-57.

Stuart-Parrigon, K. L., & Stuart, S. (2014). Perinatal depression: An update and overview. Current Psychiatry Reports, 16(9), 468. DOI: 10.1007/s11920-014-0468-6

Sun, Yuanfang. (2019). Pregnancy-specific anxiety and elective cesarean section in primiparas: A cohort study in China. PMID: 31091276 PMCID: PMC6519904 DOI: 10.1371/journal.pone.0216870

Susan Forward (2013). Mothers Who Can't Love A Healing Guide for Daughters. Harper Collins.

Takahashi, K. (1990). Examining the Strange Situation procedure with Japanese infants: Does the USA procedure work in Japan? Developmental Psychology, 26(1), 19–33.

Tiffany Field (2018). Postnatal anxiety prevalence, predictors and effects on development: A narrative review. Infant Behav Dev. 2018 May:51:24-32. doi: 10.1016/j.infbeh.2018.02.005.

Tronick, E. (1978). The Still-Face Paradigm. Developmental Psychology, 14(1), 1–12.

Tronick, E. Z., Als, H., Adamson, L., Wise, S., & Brazelton, T. B. (1978). The infant's response to entrapment between contradictory messages in face-to-face interaction. Journal of the American Academy of Child Psychiatry, 17(1), 1–13. DOI: 10.1016/S0002-7138(09)62273-1

van der Kolk, B. A. (2014). The Body Keeps the Score: Brain, Mind, and Body in the Healing of Trauma. Viking.

van Jzendoorn, M. H., & Bakermans-Kranenburg, M. J. (2019). Bridges across the intergenerational transmission of attachment gap. Current Opinion in Psychology, 25, 31-36.

Vincent, C., & Ball, S. J. (2007). Childcare, choice and class practices: Middle-class parents and their children. Routledge.

Warren, S. L., Huston, L., Egeland, B., & Sroufe, L. A. (2003). Child and Adolescent Anxiety Disorders and Early Attachment. Journal of the American Academy of Child & Adolescent Psychiatry, 42(3), 338-345.

Widom, C. S., Czaja, S. J., & Dutton, M. A. (2007). Childhood victimization and lifetime revictimization. Child Abuse & Neglect, 31(7), 725–746. DOI: 10.1016/j.chiabu.2007.02.011

Widom, C. S., White, H. R., Czaja, S. J., & Marmorstein, N. R. (2007). Long-term effects of child abuse and neglect on alcohol use and excessive drinking in middle adulthood. Journal of Studies on Alcohol and Drugs, 68(3), 317–326.

World Health Organization. (2021). Violence against women prevalence estimates, 2018. Available at: WHO Violence Against Women 2021

Yehuda, R. (2002). Post-traumatic stress disorder. The New England Journal of Medicine, 346(2), 108–114. DOI: 10.1056/NEJMra012941

Yim, I. S., Tanner Stapleton, L. R., Guardino, C. M., Hahn-Holbrook, J., & Dunkel Schetter, C. (2015). Biological and psychosocial predictors of postpartum depression: Systematic review and call for integration. Annual Review of Clinical Psychology, 11, 99–137. DOI: 10.1146/annurev-clinpsy-101414-020426

About the Author

Dr. Bandara Bandaranayake completed his B.Ed. (Honors) Degree and MPhil Degree at the University of Colombo, Sri Lanka, and earned his PhD from Monash University, Australia, on a Monash Graduate Scholarship.

After completing his first degree, Dr. Bandaranayake joined the Ministry of Education in Sri Lanka, where he served as a secondary school teacher before advancing to senior administrative roles in the Education Service. Following his PhD and a brief tenure at Monash University, he transitioned to the public service. Over the course of three decades, he held senior positions at the Department of Internal Affairs (New Zealand), the Department of Innovation, Industry and Regional Development (Australia), and the Department of Education and Early Childhood Development (Australia).

Dr. Bandaranayake's research interests span evolutionary psychology, educational psychology, cultural anthropology, educational governance, ethics and integrity, public sector reforms, and public policy. He has authored several books and numerous journal articles in these fields.

Currently, Dr. Bandaranayake is engaged in psychotherapy practice and independent research, continuing to contribute to his areas of expertise with a focus on both theoretical insights and practical applications.

Email: bandaranayakeb@gmail.com

Author's Psychotherapy Practice

Evolving Mindz
Psychotherapy, Clinical Hypnotherapy & Counselling. Melbourne, Australia

Dr Bandara Bandaranayake, B.Ed. (Hons.), MPhil, PhD
Professional Member of the Australia & New Zealand Mental Health Association, and Clinical Member of the Australian Hypnotherapists Association.

Services Offered:
- ◇ Overcome anxiety and depression,
- ◇ Heal trauma and PTSD,
- ◇ Overcome phobias and panic attacks,
- ◇ Life Coaching & Performance Coaching,
- ◇ Resolve marriage & relationship issues,
- ◇ Boost confidence & self-esteem.

Zoom and Face-to-Face Sessions Available:
- Website: www.evolvingmindz.com
- WhatsApp: +61 423 390 134
- (Eastern Standard Time - UTC/GMT +11 hours)
- Email: evolvingmindz1@gmail.com

Please visit our website or contact us via WhatsApp or email.

www.ingramcontent.com/pod-product-compliance
Lightning Source LLC
Chambersburg PA
CBHW072103020426
42334CB00017B/1613